THE LEGO MOVIE

21ˢᵀ CENTURY FILM ESSENTIALS

Cinema has a storied history, but its story is far from over. 21ˢᵗ Century Film Essentials offers a lively chronicle of cinema's second century, examining the landmark films of our ever-changing moment. Each book makes a case for the importance of a particular contemporary film for artistic, historical, or commercial reasons. The twenty-first century has already been a time of tremendous change in filmmaking the world over, from the rise of digital production and the ascent of the multinational blockbuster to increased vitality in independent filmmaking and the emergence of new voices and talents both on screen and off. The films examined here are the ones that embody and exemplify these changes, crystallizing emerging trends or pointing in new directions. At the same time, they are films that are informed by and help refigure the cinematic legacy of the previous century, showing how film's past is constantly reimagined and rewritten by its present. These are films both familiar and obscure, foreign and domestic; they are new but of lasting value. This series is a study of film history in the making. It is meant to provide a different kind of approach to cinema's story—one written in the present tense.

Donna Kornhaber, *Series Editor*

The LEGO Movie

Dana Polan

UNIVERSITY OF TEXAS PRESS ⌄ AUSTIN

Requests for permission to reproduce material from
this work should be sent to:
    Permissions
    University of Texas Press
    P.O. Box 7819
    Austin, TX 78713-7819
    utpress.utexas.edu/rp-form

♾ The paper used in this book meets the minimum requirements
of ANSI/NISO Z39.48-1992 (R1997) (Permanence of Paper).

Library of Congress Cataloging-in-Publication Data

Names: Polan, Dana B., author.
Title: The LEGO movie / Dana Polan.
Description: First edition. | Austin : University of Texas Press, 2020. |
Series: 21st century film essentials | Includes bibliographical references
    and index.
Identifiers: LCCN 2020005320 (print) | LCCN 2020005321 (ebook)
    ISBN 978-1-4773-2157-7 (paperback)
    ISBN 978-1-4773-2158-4 (ebook other)
    ISBN 978-1-4773-2159-1 (ebook)
Subjects: LCSH: LEGO movie (Motion picture) | Motion pictures—
    Production and direction—United States. | Animated films—
    History and criticism. | LEGO toys.
Classification: LCC PN1997.2.L4548 P65 2020 (print) |
    LCC PN1997.2.L4548 (ebook) | DDC 791.43/72—dc23
LC record available at https://lccn.loc.gov/2020005320
LC ebook record available at https://lccn.loc.gov/2020005321

doi:10.7560/321577

Por Leo, mi amor.

Contents

Prologue **1**

The World of Animation and the Animation of the World **7**

The LEGO Movie as Savvy Cinema **17**

Through the Rabbit Hole, into the LEGO-Verse **32**

Falling into Narrative **45**

The Extraordinary Ordinariness of LEGO **56**

The Secret Life of Toys **76**

Production History, Part 1:
  Project Development as LEGO Goes to the Movies **98**

Production History, Part 2: *The Animation Process* **117**

Production History, Part 3: *The Screenwriter-Directors* **134**

Reception and After-Life **159**

Coda **171**

Acknowledgments **173**
Notes **176**
LEGO Bibliography **199**
Index **201**

THE LEGO MOVIE

Prologue

How might we grasp the LEGO brick? The question offers itself first at a literal level: what might we do manually with that pure, modern—and pretty small—piece of plastic? Should we heed official instructions on what to build from it (and how), or follow our own playful desires to create capricious concoctions that adhere to no rules? Or shall we turn play into dis-play, permanently attaching the brick to other pieces in order to craft something fixed and final (with glue perhaps, as depicted in *The LEGO Movie* from 2014)?

The literal question tips then into more conceptual ones. What are LEGO for, why do they matter? (It is common to use "LEGO" without an "s" to refer to LEGO pieces in the plural. I'll respect that convention here.) What happens when we set out to grasp not the physical brick per se but LEGO as an idea, an icon of modernity, an image, maybe even a moving image? To what extent can the LEGO brick fit into the multimedia landscape of popular culture, especially film culture, today?

To get started, let's approach LEGO, from thing to film, through two telling quotations. The first comes from that cultural chameleon, David Bowie, so aware of his self-constructed image that he talks famously of himself here in third person: "Bowie was never meant to be. He's like a LEGO kit. I'm convinced I wouldn't like him, because he's too vacuous and undisciplined. There is no definitive David Bowie."[1] The quotation emphasizes LEGO as constantly transformative: ultimately, there is no there there since identity can be anything and can be anywhere. The brick has its own irreducible being (but one that's all surface—"vacuous," as Bowie would have it), but when it enters into combinations, all fixity of identity is left behind. LEGO constantly morph and, evidently for Bowie, *not* in a good way.

Toying with Ziggy Stardust

Yet it is possible to turn Bowie's negative valences around into playful virtues: the very genericness of the LEGO brick might be imagined to contain inventive potential and promise, its geometric purity and lack of singular identity encouraging open paths to permutation and possibility and play. For example, the idea of *The LEGO Movie* had its inception when Warner Bros. producer Dan Lin saw how, as he told me in an email, his five-year-old son "built these elaborate LEGO builds without using instructions (free building) and talked about them after he built them." As Lin recounts, he realized that his son was fictioning a story that went beyond what was physically in front of him.[2]

Lin was impressed that his son's constructions inspired and implied so much play and plotting beyond what was there concretely. In particular, as the idea for a LEGO movie percolated, Lin seemed to relish the challenge of building character-driven narrative from something that basically lacked character and fundamentally implied no specific narrative course of action. In Lin's words to the *Hollywood Reporter*, "The whole idea with LEGO bricks is that they're a blank slate that lets you create your own story."[3]

Warner Bros. already had licensed some of its iconic heroes, like Batman and Harry Potter, for LEGO box sets and LEGO video games (and in 2007 the studio had actually bought Traveller's Tales, the digital company behind these video games often based on franchised characters). Now, the Warner Animation Group's projected first feature film, *The LEGO Movie*, would center on a miniature figure (*minifig*, in LEGO parlance), Emmet, who had no backstory. His identity would be the generic one of urban construction worker (in fact, one of the earliest and most common, in many senses of the word, minifigs), and yet he would nonetheless prove himself the stuff of legend, worthy of sagas narrated about him (including *The LEGO Movie* itself). Even Bowie had had to admit that we can be heroes, if just for one day.

My second quotation comes from the sequel to *The LEGO Movie, The LEGO Movie 2: The Second Part* from 2019: "It's all just the expression of the death of imagination in the subconscious of an adolescent," asserts Rex, a universe-trotting adventurer minifig who seemed initially a good guy, beholden to none of the powers that be. Rex had declared earlier that Emmet's adventures (as chronicled in the first film) indeed made the construction worker a hero in the eyes of many. Rex,

The Chosen One?

however, ultimately reveals himself to be the film's bad guy and makes his statement to Emmet to undercut the latter's confidence in the rich vitality of his LEGO universe. Probably no declaration goes so far in pinpointing the kind of interpretative language a scholar also might use in analyzing the films' meanings, and probably few films go so far in offering such an assertion while ultimately making fun of it.

In line with Rex's contention, the famous LEGO "System of Play" (plastic elements that when combined lead to larger constructions) has sometimes been taken to task, especially with the rise of box sets including instructions that push children (as well as so-called "Adult Fans of LEGO") toward preset ends, as discouraging deep imagination and free play. Rex's accusation is not totally off the mark.

Yet it's not totally accurate either, from what we see of adolescent play in both the sequel and its predecessor. Rex, after all, has hardened himself to fun and can't be expected to appreciate the full richness of the universe he assails. Finn, the young boy we see playing with LEGO in *The LEGO Movie*, along with sister Bianca in the sequel, are not at all about slavishly following set paths and instead use LEGO for quite imaginative play (which, from the first to second film, is ever more expansive, Bianca bringing in more and more components, including ones beyond LEGO itself). It's not so much about "the death of imagination" as about its emphatic celebration, with, as we'll see in the sequel, upbeat music as the ultimate organizing force behind it. Imagination, or its dearth and its death. In a strong way, in fact, everything we see of LEGO life in both movies is ultimately to be attributed to the imagination of humans, presumably like us, whose creative efforts we are witnessing as LEGO minifig Emmet and cohort go through their adventures. It is worth noting that Rex in *The LEGO Movie 2: The Second Part* is in fact a version of Emmet from the future. That the film's knowing, "academic" critique actually comes from an alternative Emmet matters for the ways the film's seeming naiveté masks a deeper sophistication, yet a sophistication that twists around on itself to insist on pure playfulness after all.[4]

This is the space LEGO move in, and it's the space *The LEGO Movie* will play emphatically and knowingly with—in several senses of "play." The film is visually inventive in a way that references LEGO, yet shows feature animation reaching for new heights of creativity in a digital age where play is often less about physical manipulation of things (the hard brick, for instance) than, at best, either the manipulation of a joystick controller that makes virtual things move or the vicarious experience of watching a movie where movement and action have been fabricated for us.

In the following pages, after some broad initial thoughts on the predominant role animated films have come to play in today's movie culture, my study moves in closely to *The LEGO Movie* itself to account for the experience of it directly *as a movie*—one whose particular stylistic and narrative qualities merit analysis and description in depth. But to clarify that particularity, I'll also move outward to the larger context of animated films that specifically narrate what happens when toys come to life (and often are made to promote the sale of such playthings in a real world where they are bereft of such life). *The LEGO Movie* works with a tradition of animation that reflects on animation, but it does so, as I'll argue, in unique fashion. Once we've seen in these ways what is so special in form and content about *The LEGO Movie*, I'll chronicle its production history from the story of the LEGO company's involvement with moving-image culture to the development of outsourced animation in Australia (where *The LEGO Movie* was animated) to the career trajectory of *The LEGO Movie* writer-director-producers Phil Lord and Chris Miller. Lord and Miller have long displayed a love of satire, free play, and the mix of high-culture reference with lowbrow humor, and these qualities are amply on display in *The LEGO Movie*. The film extends the LEGO brand even as it toys with it (pun intended). To inquire, then, into the place of LEGO in film culture requires that we move back and forth between LEGO as physical things and as the less-embodied image they become when they flit across the movie screen.

The World of Animation and the Animation of the World

It often seems as if the cartoon—and the cartoonish, perhaps—are everywhere today as veritably the mainstream of Hollywood entertainment. Once limited to the special-occasion Disney feature (and rare rivals to it), and then for a long time the province of kids watching Saturday morning network cartoons and later, specialty channels (for example, Nickelodeon Jr.), animation passed through the realm of snarky adult fare on evening cable (Adult Swim, for instance, itself owned by Warner Bros.) or outlier networks (FOX, especially, whose modern success in many ways can be pegged to *The Simpsons*) to stand at the center of big-budget, big-effects Hollywood entertainment. To give just one set of figures, in studying box office take for animated films across the history of cinema, two scholars of global industries found that more animated features were made in the ten-year period from 1997 to 2006 than in the entire history of animation up to then.[1] The situation has only amplified in the years since.

Depending on who you are and what you think cinema should be at its best, this is either a great thing or a sign of the art form's decline. Famously, or infamously according to one's

point of view, philosopher Stanley Cavell argued that each
photographed frame in a live-action film offers a transcription
of reality, adding up to what he termed the "world viewed,"
a position that led him to demote animation, with its use of
drawings, to a position outside cinema's claims to artistic and
cultural importance. In his blanket condemnation, "Cartoons
are *not* movies."[2]

Conversely, some defenders of animation today don't merely
argue that it's not some sort of marginal form or degradation
of cinema's true artistic potential but instead claim boldly that
animation sums up the essence of cinema—that it may bring
out what we might call its fundamental nature. In the digital
age especially, they argue, animation realizes cinema: it severs connections to external reality and offers instead created
worlds—worlds that, as the very term "animation" implies,
imagine fantastically the giving of life to things.

In contrast with Cavell's notorious preemption of animation
from the art of cinema, proponents for animation's creative
potential like to quote digital theorist Lev Manovich's equally
famous (or equally infamous) declaration that "digital cinema is a particular case of animation"—in other words, that
animation's ability to leave photographic reality behind is its
fundamental condition and, indeed, defines filmic creation per
se today.[3]

To be sure, to take the example at hand, *The LEGO Movie*
pretends visually to be giving us not digitalization but photographic stop-motion animation to the point of keeping some
of the jitteriness of that mode of moviemaking. It stands as
a visual construction built up through artifice, yet it mimes
a world viewed through photographic reproduction. And it
is noteworthy how big-budget feature animation remains

indebted to a visual style that approximates realism through centered composition, classical perspective, continuity editing, narrative, and emphasis on character. In mainstream features, for instance, pure flights of fancy into abstraction are often held in check by character-driven narrative and, indeed, by the emphasis on character itself. To take just one instance, from 1941, the "Pink Elephants" delirium in one sequence of *Dumbo* is explained as a hallucination the titular protagonist has, and the breakdown of logic and visual reason is thereby contained to the one scene rather than spreading throughout.

Perhaps, in fact, by avoiding full abstraction, mainstream animation makes fantastical transformation all the more impactful. Digitalization can at the extreme take us away from something that looks like our reality into pure realms of visual invention, but the persistence of traces of our world, under all the transformation, gives resonance and relevance to the morphing.

Animation offers fabrications, constructed worlds of the imagination, fictions of artificiality and fantastic design. Images break from reality and, significantly, come to constitute a new reality in their own right. And they do so in an age where, beyond the movie theater per se, built worlds, projected images, and media practices of all sorts surround us, often suggesting that the reality—or multiple realities—that matter are the ones that appear on all the screens we live in, and through, in our overwhelmed society of the spectacle.

It's easy then to imagine that there is no space that hasn't been mediatized, coopted, manipulated, or constructed, from the cities around us to the media messages we hold in our heads to even our very being—which in moments of paranoid fantasy we can imagine as having been fabricated elsewhere, by others: this is the central premise of *Blade Runner* or *The Truman Show* or *The Matrix* but also, to a degree, of *The LEGO Movie*.[4] And this sense that we are the playthings or puppets of powerful figures who can exert their force on us from afar—and even determine our life force—has its direct political correlate: the sentiment or suspicion that who we are, what sort of lives we are enabled to have, the opportunities afforded to us (or not), are decided by power brokers often situated at great distances from us but whose effects are close up. Yet, at the same time, there's also a hard-to-break fascination with those very workings of power among the ordinary citizens potentially most damaged by it: in our media age, power exists itself as dynamic visuality, as media spectacle, and it can dazzle and fascinate even as it oppresses. The aptly named President Business of *The LEGO Movie* (eventually renaming himself as "Lord" Business) offers in his very being a marriage of top-down politics and capitalist enterprise that relies on the seductions of the image to support its offensives into everyday life and everyday consciousness. Released two years before an orange-haired megalomaniac, veritably a media construction in his own right (a former reality-TV star), came to presidential power in the United States, *The LEGO Movie* could seem scarily prescient in its depiction of orange-haired President Business as a megalomaniac who hides truths through media manipulation to such a degree that everyday LEGO citizens become lulled by the complacencies of post-truthiness.

One converse, though, of the paranoid nightmare that everything you do—and even everything you are—has been fabricated by others, is the fantasy that if everything is a construct, you need simply to change existing terms to become different

A leader who claims "great and unmatched wisdom" for himself

enough to escape the current situation (just as LEGO in the physical world and in the movie can endlessly transform). A click of the computer mouse, for instance, can take you somewhere else, the hyperlink to a new page functioning like the leap into hyperspace in science-fiction film. If everything is manipulated image, then everything can be further modified: we live in the fantasy of border crossings and of mutability. If animation and comics and superheroes have come to constitute the core of Hollywood cinema, their conjuncture is all about fantasies of transformation, reworkings of identity, remakings of destiny.[5]

It is noteworthy, for instance, how many mainstream films, live-action as well as animated, are about narrative lines being reshaped, eventualities being undone, characters being rebuilt. For instance, in time-travel plots (which, as the late film scholar Thomas Elsaesser noted, have in recent years been much more about journeying into a past to right a wrong history than about voyaging to a not-yet-unfolded future),[6] narrative itself has no absolute inevitability: any story can fork down a different path than the one it started out on. (The sequel to *The LEGO Movie* plays centrally with this conceit.)

Even beyond the direct fantasies of science fiction, so much popular culture works today in a "what-if" mode, and, once again, the fantasy that it could all be different—or have gone differently—has a direct political correlate in times when many people often want to believe that recent history is a bad dream, a joke, a media construct or a "reality show" conceit gone horribly wrong (but is—hopefully—correctible).

A comment by media historian Shawna Kidman in her 2019 book about the omnipresence of comic adaptations in today's Hollywood could well be extended to feature animation—"Its success in that corporate sphere [of merchandising and branding] and its reputation as a go-to source for big-budget Hollywood projects have made the medium mainstream, a kind of playground for big shots with money to burn."[7] Indeed, key factors that Kidman sees for comic films gaining priority in the new Hollywood also are determinant for animation: for example, the increasing sophistication of CGI technology, which makes possible ever more impactful spectacle; the ability of such spectacle to work across the globe (superheroes and animation have worldwide appeal); and the great potential for tie-ins and ancillary marketing.[8] Animation here offers easily recognizable and brandable characters who can translate across cultures *and across generations*.

This last point is worth lingering on for a moment. There no doubt is much truth to the assertion that a great deal of animation is for kids only, and across moving-image history, both film and television, we find a recurrence of cartoons that have the youngest of children as their target and make few concessions to the adult viewer. But the big-budget animated feature, to get the crowd, increasingly needs to go for more than the toddler audience. Even a movie for the youngest viewer may gesture to the adult guardian along for the ride. For instance, the 2017 feature film adaptation of the My Little Pony toy franchise gives the sidekick ponies a bit of snark and up-to-dateness (one pony talks of "multitasking") to add sophistication to an initially infantile franchise that revels in squeaky prepubescent voices, sugary glitter and gleam, perky optimism, and so on, but that increasingly also accepts adult viewers and intentionally plays to them as well. In the specific case of My Little Pony, there's even a term to acknowledge the phenomenon of children's culture that is also simultaneously adult: "Brony." The term offers a mash-up of "Bro" and "Pony," since Bronies are overwhelmingly grown-up *guys* who relish, sometimes with irony but sometimes without, this brand of kid culture.

In today's blockbuster, cross-platform media landscape, culture needs to be sold across generations, and this is best achieved when an offering to children also resonates with parents. As Derek Johnson shows in a study of cross-generational media products, this often can happen when the commodity up for sale (whether a toy or moving-image adaptation) has been around for a while: new iterations of the commodity reach out to the most recent generations of kids while their parents can also be drawn in by nostalgia for something they remember from their own childhoods. To take an immediate example, one that Johnson devotes some pages to, there are now generations upon generations who have played with LEGO and continue to do so, as in the striking phenomenon of Adult Fans of LEGO, for whom everything from the feel of the plastic to the clicks of connection among pieces to the building up and building down of worlds possesses long-term resonance, which they relish passing on to their kids.[9]

To the charges of infantilization often directed against cartoon films, and in fact against a cinema, both live and animated, of diversion, fantasy, and escape—charges that from the 1970s on were as much political as aesthetic (mainstream cinema in the age of Reagan, and after, was said to be all about dumbing down to make us accept a bad political situation by benumbing us to it)—we could as easily argue an adultification of popular culture in which serious concerns enter into seemingly light entertainment. To be sure—as, say, PBS's Barney might bear witness—there is probably a lower-age threshold of popular diversion that fantasizes pure and innocent worlds of saccharine simplicity. (Yet, to take a famous example, mature concerns can creep in as, across generations, viewers continue to bear the trauma of the death of Bambi's mother.) But today, with social media and the ubiquity of screens bringing the world into children's lives (including a world of violence, as in school shootings and the need now to train for their eventuality; of sexuality, as in very public scandals about politicians' adultery imbroglios; of sexual violence, as in front-page reports of harassment by figures even at the very top of political and economic power; and so on), oases of innocence are harder to maintain, and a popular culture that isn't alert to such pressures of the outside world can seem anachronistic, quaint even, the sort of sugary escapism many of today's kids wouldn't be caught dead indulging in. It's not simply, as some scholars from the 1970s on have noted, that individual works of popular culture differentially target a range of generations, getting at adults through in-jokes that will pass over the kids' heads.[10] Today's popular culture often assumes a degree of adultness within the child.[11] There's even an acronym for this in the world of toy marketing: KGOY—Kids Getting Older Younger!

For all its imputed focus on diverting kids and giving them a nice sugary treat, mainstream animation can be trafficking in some pretty heavy and pretty heady stuff, albeit in playful mode. And it can often be quite explicit about this: for example, *The LEGO Movie 2* makes not merely time travel but also erudite discussion of its potential philosophical conundrums central to its narrative (for instance, what would happen if you met another version of yourself?), while *Spider-Man: Into the Spider-Verse* luxuriates (visually as well as narratively) in parallel universes and what-if possibilities that might ensue if one could switch from one particular existence to another. And *The LEGO Movie* is itself, of course, all about destiny (but also the possibility of forking from it); about mutability of identity (but also about finding you have no ultimate control over your own being, manipulated as it is by others); about realizing you may have no subjectivity or will of your own (but maybe you can still become a hero); about power at a distance (but also flights from it); about the benumbing effects of the Culture Industry; about the interweave of creativity and collectivity; and so on.

And yet. . . . we should be wary of turning playful animation into nothing but sheer philosophy. Animation's severing of the bonds to physical reality makes it of necessity a comment, sometimes explicit and sometimes not, on the power of images to enthrall us, especially ones created top-down for our mass entertainment. But that severing itself diverts and fascinates and awes in ways that seem less about deep meanings (allegorical or otherwise) than about the sheer pleasure of open-ended, fantastical seeing in image-saturated times. We buy into the plays of sight across the screens of our daily lives, and movies serve as one key aspect of this visual delight. What's particularly compelling in this respect about *The LEGO Movie* is how aware it shows itself to be of such concerns. It is a movie that is savvy about the ways digitalization, by its nature, raises some big questions about image and identity; the means by which digitalization awes us with the fantasy of seemingly pure and diverting ways of seeing; and the manner in which popular entertainment itself works between politics and pleasure and holds the two together in our cultural moment.

The LEGO Movie as Savvy Cinema

The end credits for *The LEGO Movie* go on for over seven and a half minutes, listing scores of craftspeople, accountants, and so on (including *thirteen* executive producers). No doubt, extensive, seemingly endless, credits are par for the course in today's special-effects-driven, CGI-derived blockbuster Hollywood entertainment cinema, and *The LEGO Movie* in fact isn't excessive in the amount of time given over to its credits (the numbers go up a bit, though, if we also include the opening logos of all the production/distribution/finance companies involved). To take another example, *Spider-Man: Into the Spider-Verse*, a later feature animation supervised by the directors of *The LEGO Movie*, has over ten minutes of credits (although the later film involved many more animation styles than its predecessor, which pushed up the number of animators and related craftspeople and laborers). The very commonness of long credit sequences in such big-budget, effects-laden films as these tells us a lot about how labor-intensive (but also managerial-intensive) mainstream moviemaking has become. (It's purely coincidental but noteworthy, perhaps, that the length of the credits for *The LEGO Movie* approximates the *full length* of the cartoons that accompanied feature films during the studio era.)[1]

The many lines to "below-the-line" craft

But in the case of *The LEGO Movie*, the fact that so many people had to come together to fabricate this work of popular culture can seem more than a bit curious since the very idea of the movie—and of the toy it derives from—has centrally to do with going your own way, cultivating your own individual talent, discovering your own fount of creative potential, and so on, rather than taking up a slot in a corporatized work-world, no matter the specialized talent you might bring to the large-scale task before you. LEGO are supposed to be about that little brick you hold in your hand and then craft imaginative possibilities from. That's supposed to be free from the pressures of mass enterprise.

The LEGO Movie celebrates the potential inner spirit of each individual—and pits it against the numbing dictatorship of the aptly named Lord Business. Yet, tellingly, when David C. Robertson describes the managerial turnaround in 2004 that reined in the rampant diversification of divisions within the LEGO company, he could be describing Lord Business's dictatorial style in which inviolate rules are passed from on high to an array of micro-managers and white-collar information gatherers and data processors, and in which the man at the top seems to have his finger on everything (as when Business checks in on ad campaigns, radio broadcasts, television shows, and so on while striding forcefully through corporate headquarters). The "first priority," Robertson notes, "was to restore discipline and direction. And that would come only from a series of goals passed down through a chain of command. . . . While the company has been aggressively hiring diverse and creative people, it's also recruited people whose primary responsibility is to bring focus and discipline to all that creative energy."[2]

The LEGO Movie itself is a work of big business: made by one of the most behemoth media companies (Time Warner, recently absorbed into ATT and renamed WarnerMedia) to promote the product of one of the most behemoth toy companies, The LEGO Group (hereafter, TLG). Yet the plot of *The LEGO Movie* is to a very large degree about getting away from corporate control and following your own path to greatness (greatness, moreover, defined as being true to your own potential, available to anyone and everyone, to invent and to fashion creative possibility—greatness, then, as something other than excellence: just creative capacity, no matter what comes from it).

As it works itself out in the movie, we can term such contradictions *Irony* and, as we'll see, it's only one of the many ironies that *The LEGO Movie* explicitly and readily embraces. Importantly, it's irony that's even ironic about itself, what I will term a "disarming irony" that calls every position into question and ends up standing fully and finally for no fixed take on things.

It is yet another mark of this ironic knowingness to that popular culture which deflates anything serious (both in what the film itself says and in what we, as commentators on it, might want to say about it), that after I wrote my lines above about the film's necessarily contradictory investment in lengthy credits, I saw the sequel, *The LEGO Movie 2: The Second Part* (even its title can't resist joking with itself), and discovered that this savvy franchise had anticipated my very analysis: this time around, the end credits are scored in part to a song about how the credits are often the best moments of a movie and how you need to stay through them!

Along with its sequel, *The LEGO Movie* comes off as a knowing and aware work of culture that accepts and enjoys its own ambivalences. In its consummate cultivation of such irony, *The LEGO Movie* stands as essential to key directions in popular film today. It is a distinctive work of animation (in its case, using computer methods to render digital images that appear quite photographic and thereby deliberately pre-digital) standing out in a time when animation has seemingly become omnipresent within the landscape of Hollywood entertainment. Along with other key cases of feature animation, it shows how the charge that these are just "cartoons" no longer fits. Like the blockbuster live-action films that also seem so prevalent today, it is big on high speed and explosive action (chases, shoot-outs, and things blowing up, all mirrored in a frenetic style of fast edits and quick "camera" movement) and delivers on high-octane popular entertainment, yet it adds to the vibrancy notable moments of deliberate, and deliberative, calm in which big questions about life's purpose are analyzed.[3] And yet (to add another twist), it deflates its own seriousness through the disarming irony that keeps popping in to mock that very seriousness, which the film often initially asks us to take quite seriously indeed.

The movie celebrates creative play: it's all about mixing and mashing up universes and resisting an older generation that feels there's one right way to do things and that everything needs to be fixed in place. But this celebration is all in the commercial cause of a toy that increasingly can, because of the tie-ins between media company and toy company, be all about following instructions, hewing to the declared correct path, and building things according to a predetermined outcome. To take a salient example, one we'll return to, when LEGO first got involved with the movies in a big way, it was through a licensing of Star Wars characters and gizmos. As any parent who buys their kids LEGO knows, from that point on, such LEGO kits centered increasingly on pre-formed larger pieces— such as a starship's body—that might only be built upon in constrained, guided ways, especially if one's goal was to construct something from a venerated film. In fact, fans of the movies that led to licensed sets (which soon came to include other franchises, like Harry Potter) often wanted to follow instructions slavishly with pre-formed pieces that pointed the way to the canonic model that would stand as the endpoint of the process, and that would thereby enable close re-creation of an icon from the movies, rather than a random invention that went off-script.[4] (At the same time, we need to be attentive to the possibilities of creativity even with kits: as two friends, each with two boys, told me, their kids would follow the instructions the first time around and then everything would go into a big bin with elements from previous kits, and the amalgam would be dipped into for more open-ended constructions beyond printed instructions.)

The sheer quantity of acknowledgments in the credits belies any sense of LEGO, and of *The LEGO Movie*, as pure celebration of DIY amateur initiative. Indeed, whatever inventiveness is celebrated here in the movie comes only because it was made by a big team and had such a big infrastructure. Under the end credits we do for an instant see short bits from some home LEGO movies that were contributed to a competition for ordinary fans, but these are themselves given minimal credit as "Additional Content" and simply pass by as part of a flow of images that from start to finish is all about throwing lots of (admittedly compelling) imagery at the spectator and celebrating the power of corporate art-making in doing so. The DIY videos (the fuller versions of which are available as supplementary material on the DVD) are framed within the larger accomplishment of *The LEGO Movie* as *mass* work of culture, and they become one more piece in its assemblage, one more spectacle that passes before our eyes as the film celebrates, with the credits, its own massive accomplishments.

No doubt, the very number of credits for *The LEGO Movie* (it's now as if every below-the-line craftsperson rightfully gets recognition) acknowledges specialization and diversity. Usefully, the credits remind us that the popular art of mass culture isn't pegged to the singular vision of individual auteurs. And it may well be the case that big teams of creative personnel can foster artistic initiative by allowing every inventive avenue to be explored, with everyone encouraged to do their part, once they are provided with enough infrastructure to do so. *The LEGO Movie* may have had a lot of people working on it, but the results are in their own fashion quite innovative, even experimental, offering a unique visual style that belies any sense of blockbuster Hollywood as itself a monolith of mass conformity. *The LEGO Movie* is, for instance, part of a trend of films offering new alternatives to or within the dominant styles of computer animation, opening them up (such as *Spider-Man: Into the Spider-Verse*, which appears to mimic an array of animation styles, predigital as well as digital), and thereby responding perhaps to a fatigue setting in with standard computer animation, now that it's becoming something of a tradition. The fact that *The LEGO Movie* mimics stop-motion animation (but through computer technique) by simulating a jerky frame-rate is noteworthy in this respect as a craft attempt to evoke modes of production before digitalization.[5]

The LEGO Movie seems to participate in the synergies of salesmanship—a toy becomes a movie that sells more toys *and* games *and* books *and* theme park experiences *and* on and on—even as it critiques the top-down model of business and promotes a nonentrepreneurial mythology of being creative for its own playful sake. (Economics rears its ugly head rarely in the movie, as when Emmet, told by a barista that his latte is $37, pauses for a moment and then bursts out with "Awesome!"[6] Yet every frame of the film radiates the money that went into it, and that is confirmed by the lengthy credits.)

Such ironies as this—the corporate invocation of individualized noncorporatized initiative—can then be embraced by corporate Hollywood at large, which easily celebrates mass production as folk artistry. For instance, the film's hit song "Everything Is Awesome" (about which more later) is introduced, in the narrative of the film, as a regularized and even monotonously annoying robotic ode to conformity that would seem to stand as the cloying converse of good music. (Perhaps curiously, in the DVD's special features it is the *only* even vaguely interactive element, included in a sing-along version. In other words, the one time the DVD encourages participation is in the case of manipulative music that makes one respond slavishly to the beat.) Yet—surprisingly, or maybe not so surprisingly given the ironies of mass culture today— "Everything Is Awesome" got singled out as one of the nominees for Best Song at the Oscars, recognition that some people in the movie business found it creative and catchy and worthy of celebration as "real" music. (For what it's worth, it lost to "Glory" from the civil rights film *Selma*. Yet Lord-Miller's production of "Everything Is Awesome" for the Oscars ceremony itself, complete with animation mixed with over-the-top live-action choreography that included LEGO Oscars being handed out to audience members like Oprah Winfrey, was certainly one of the winningest moments of the evening.)

Often made by creative figures who have gone to film school—or taken film classes or cultural studies courses (as co-writer and director Phil Lord jokes, maybe only partially joking, "My dream is to have terrible undergraduate term papers written about the movie")[7]—many Hollywood blockbusters don't just set out to divert but to offer a reflexive, reflective take on their own qualities as entertainment while still delivering the goods of playful diversion. As such, they threaten to disarm any critical position one could take on them since they anticipate those positions and embed them wittingly into their very narratives.

As another example of such irony from the history of popular culture (one that no doubt is one inspiration for *The LEGO Movie* within the tradition of animation), we could cite *The Simpsons*, where the tension between corporatism and nonconformity often plays itself out through the show's frequent cynicism about the very beliefs corporate parent FOX extols on its right-wing news shows. *The Simpsons* is, of course, famous for the capaciousness of its critique of contemporary culture: every thing comes up for derision, including, predictably perhaps, LEGO's ambivalent role in DIY creativity. Law-and-media scholars Dan Hunter and Julian Thomas, who have written cogently on LEGO's tenacious defense of its intellectual property, concisely summarize a scene in the FOX show (season 23, episode 11) that deals cannily with precisely that increasing emphasis on licensed kits, heavy on rules and instructions so as to lead to iconic objects and decors from fan-revered films like *Star Wars*: "Lisa visits her local 'Blocko' store, but is disappointed to find only an array of sets dedicated to scenes or characters from the Cosmic Wars franchise. 'I kind of wanted to create my own thing,' she says; 'do you sell any just plain sets?' 'No. We do all the imagining for you,' says the helpful woman behind the counter. Lisa picks up a 'Chubba the Shedd's Dust Palace' box: 'I'll just buy one of these and build something different.' The salesperson responds: 'Do, and you better build yourself a lawyer.'"[8]

In the tradition of animated self-aware irony, *The LEGO Movie* has also to do with the ways it handles such tensions within its narrative (and not just, say, as discussed above, between the narrative and its production context as signaled in the credits). Unlike the heartfelt lessons about letting go of childhood attachments in, for instance, the *Toy Story* or *How to Train Your Dragon* franchises, *The LEGO Movie* proffers meaningful themes and messages *only to then render them silly through wisecracking, knowing deflation*. There are, for instance, any number of speechifying moments in *The LEGO Movie* in which someone stands up for creativity, individuality, the potential in all of us, and so on, but each of these is undercut by a knowing and deliberate jokiness. To take just one example, when Vitruvius (voiced by the portentous Morgan

Freeman), the spiritual mentor to the protagonist Emmet, tells his pupil that he needs to "*Believe*," he then immediately acknowledges that this homily sounds like something from a cat poster. (Later, when, in a moment of extreme challenge, Emmet remembers the lesson, he is literally in front of a cat poster whose feline comes to life and restates the lesson in Vitruvius/Freeman's voice.)

The essential wisdom of cats

If we wanted, we could call this not just Irony, but Postmodernism—a case of popular culture eschewing or jettisoning deep meaning for the sake of sheer game and self-deconstructing jokiness. Here, visual (and aural) play flits up before the spectator and then moves away (here's meaningfulness; now it departs by being undercut) so that the next new set of images and sounds, hovering between meaningfulness and pure surface spectacle, can flash up for an instant and then move on, and on and on. At the same time, it is worth lingering on those meaningful instances and the touching emotional moments that pop up through all the entertaining silliness, since they often can be very moving even as they're being set up to be mocked: later, *Spider-Man: Into the Spider-Verse* confirms just how possible, and powerful, it is to combine a wink-wink ironizing that deflates depth with very resonant depths of sentiment, especially around family, self-identity, the search for personal purpose, and so on.

To be sure, sentiment in *The LEGO Movie* has a representational arc across its narrative. The humans whose interactions we witness in the live-action ending don't really treat the minifigs as quasi-persons (even Finn appears to realize that Emmet is just a plaything while at the same time calling on this LEGO to be a hero), yet these humans definitely recognize their own psychodramas in the stories those minifigs are made to enact, as when Dad realizes Lord Business is the bad guy and asks what Emmet would say to him. There's a learning curve for Dad that is not only about allowing open play into his life but sentiment too. Thus, in the culminating parallel editing between Lord Business/Emmet and Dad/Finn—where Business/Dad both walk screen right to apologize—feeling is allowed to suffuse the live-action scenario. It is directly deflated only in the LEGO world itself: "We've got a hugger," Emmet says. But the deflation is there nonetheless, as the film can't seem to resist punctuating every heartfelt moment with a quick taking up of ironic distance from it.

Phil Lord and Chris Miller, the writers and directors of *The LEGO Movie* as well as the producers of *Spider-Man: Into the Spider-Verse*, traffic centrally in comic deflation, but they also are wary of any position that would freeze this into the be-all of ironic popular culture. They want the deflation *and* the meaningfulness; they want the twists that entail that we remain always in some suspended place between joke *and* resonant depth. As a form not always assured of cultural respectability, the cartoon, whether animated or in printed comics, is one place this can happen. Witness Lord and Miller's contribution to a Peter Porker comic book that came out in summer 2019: knowingly reworking a famous comics event from 2015, "Secret Wars," Lord and Miller's episode (cowritten with Marvel cartoonist Jason Latour) chronicles a battle between classic superheroes (serious ones who confront big moral and existential issues) and inevitably silly ones like Peter Porker and the infamous Howard the Duck. At a deliberate meta-level, the conflict is about approaches to comics and cartoons, and to popular culture per se: is any of this to be taken seriously, or is it all just entertaining diversion? The ironic deflation itself becomes a predictable strategy that then itself must be deflated: thus, recognizing the very absurdity of a comics character like himself, Peter Porker declares at one point, "Ain't that the whole point? Y'know that whole 'We exist to deflate the pretense of our serious counterparts' jazz.'" As every stance turns against its opposite, the only answer (not necessarily an affirmative one) the story can ultimately offer is to reboot everything and begin the process all over again: on the last page, Peter and Howard meet up anew, but each now bears some of the features of the other, as if the new jump start has taken us to a parallel universe, albeit one that is still going to go inevitably, and go on and on inevitably, in the same twisty direction.[9]

The LEGO Movie works in this self-aware tradition, one that knows, for instance, about the conventions of entertainment (and the ideological baggage these come with), that knows "postmodernism," and that knows the ins and outs of cultural critique more generally. Take as one example what we might term the "just enough" political correctness in many recent works of popular culture: they will include "just enough" feminism or "just enough" diversity to claim some progressiveness even as they ultimately defer to masculine ideologies around prowess and action heroism. As a friend to whom I mentioned the idea put it, "When did films (and popular culture more generally) start to rely on this joking contrast between the incompetent male hero and the super-competent woman who plays the helper role? The outward message is to endorse feminism by rejecting the super-competent male hero who rescues the damsel in distress, but the result is often to celebrate male entitlement—the more incompetent the hero is, the more offensive it is that he gets to be the hero in the first place. *Guardians of the Galaxy* and *Ant-Man* follow the same pattern (albeit with less irony), and I see it in commercials all the time."

The idea *might* seem applicable to *The LEGO Movie*, where Wyldstyle is a charismatic kick-ass female action figure yet gets relegated to the sidelines while the seemingly banal Emmet is declared the "special" one. *The LEGO Movie* here *might* be compared to one of its obvious inspirations, *The Matrix*, where super-action woman Trinity (Carrie-Ann Moss) starts the film in dynamic style as she acrobatically decimates an entire police squadron but where, then, the much less dynamic Neo (cast, deliberately it would seem, with the somewhat vacuous Keanu Reeves) ends up getting all the glory. But while *The Matrix* seems unaware of its own gender limitations (such as the fact that Trinity, for no apparent reason except that the plot needs it, falls in love with the bland Neo), *The LEGO Movie* appears quite savvy about its own "just enoughness": Wyldstyle is visibly miffed that Emmet came accidentally to fulfill the prophecy of a "special" one, when she clearly could have been deemed more deserving of the title, and *The LEGO Movie 2* goes so far as to have another character question her about the very fact that she seems, in the first film, to have done all the heavy work of an action hero while Emmet got the special recognition. The awareness works on several levels: within the story, it is a character commenting on gender inequality; but from outside the film, it's the filmmakers showing their own awareness of such unfairness as a common convention across many narrative works of contemporary popular culture.[10] And, no doubt, in another twist of the ironic process, it's like *The Simpsons*, say, or *South Park* in bringing in political incorrectness and letting it do its work (we do appreciate Emmet turning out to be more than an anonymous loser) even as it disavows that very incorrectness.

Wyldstyle: hero of a thousand faces?

Faced with a work of popular culture that anticipates the critiques one can bring to bear on it—and even incorporates those critiques into its very narrative—we might move beyond mere critique to context, asking why a disarming irony has become so mainstream today and what that might say about popular culture in our times. Conversely, we could also tunnel more closely into the individual work to pinpoint precisely the mechanisms and operations of irony that it engages in, seeking in this case to figure out the place of *The LEGO Movie* in our cultural present.

I hesitate to call my take on *The LEGO Movie* an *interpretation*, as I take ironic popular cinema to be all about the difficulties of thematic fixity and about a reveling instead in visual dynamics above and beyond any meaningfulness we can attach to them. With a rush of motion, *The LEGO Movie* quickly immerses the viewer in a kinetic experience that settles down only infrequently in resonant reflection—reflection, moreover, given ironic punctuation and then passed over for the next instance of visual (and aural) dynamics. It can be pretty fun. So let's jump in.

Through the Rabbit Hole, into the LEGO-Verse

We should indeed be wary of the search for deep meanings below the entertainment surface of *The LEGO Movie*. In fact, so much of what *The LEGO Movie* is "about" has to do with that surface—the sheer rush of images that bounce up for the spectator as the film soars through the forward movement (literally so) of narrative, the sheer splendor of vibrant colors and vast constructed (and deconstructed) universes.

Pulsating music that sounds like it belongs to a fantasy epic accompanies the very first images of the Warner Bros. (and Warner Animation Group) and Village Roadshow logos, announcing the genre affiliations (this will be an action saga, no matter what else might transpire), yet the very look of the titles tames that excitement by reiterating that whatever else might transpire, this is still after all a movie about plastic bricks, "mere" toys. Moreover, the logos hang down from strings, giving us a hint of the movie's ultimate big reveal but also perhaps making a first joke about the bigness of the production (major film companies are involved), yet also the smallness and simplicity of it all: it's really just simple LEGO after all, the "mini" in minifig serving as an operative conceit.

Like so many other works of contemporary entertainment cinema, *The LEGO Movie* offers itself up as a kinetic (and

Movie corporation world-making

dynamically aural) experience: this is a movie that moves. Which isn't to say that it doesn't rely also on instances of stasis: as I'll note later, directors Phil Lord and Chris Miller are quite enamored of frozen moments in which a character exhibits a slow and implacable reaction to the world around him or her. Emmet, for instance, constantly goes into a kind of immobility as he attempts to comprehend the adventure he's been thrust into—and the heroic role demanded of him. Unlike other Lord/Miller pauses, though, fleeting instances of frozenness here only bring out all the more the irony of a movie about "LEGO." These are essentially unmoving, or little-moving, toy figurines, but they are given animated life through cinema so that the moments of stasis, however temporary, become a negation of the film's animated negation of what LEGO figures are essentially all about.[1]

Wildly inventive—filled with rich puns, clever ironic dialogue, and that ever-changing and ever-dazzling visual spectacle, *The LEGO Movie* is incredibly fast-moving as it zips the viewer through a variety of universes. It often includes scenes where someone, such as Vitruvius, breathlessly enumerates characters and worlds that show the seemingly endless diversity of real LEGO products (sometimes with numbers for the parts popping up on-screen); on the one hand, such scenes could be seen as vibrant hawking of toys by the film, yet on the other hand, the scenes move so quickly they can cease to have any direct promotional purpose and serve simply to dazzle with the splendor of visual richness.

The rush of ever-changing imagery is not only about motion through space: it can happen within a static frame, as in those instances where LEGO are built and rebuilt inside the shot: for example, when Emmet first wakes up and gets ready for work, he follows the codified rituals of an instruction manual that, among other (obvious) exhortations like "Breathe," tells him to get dressed, a command that is visualized as an in-frame montage of Emmet trying on different outfits. Perhaps this could seem a kind of LEGO sales pitch that offers visually and vicariously to the spectator the fascinating diversity that can be had with real, buyable LEGO pieces. Constantly, predictably, as indeed might befit a branded film that one imagines is supposed to promote physical LEGO toys, *The LEGO Movie* shows off LEGO. Yet throughout, the montages that portray LEGO quick-change are often very quick indeed (and actually include some made-up options that are not really available for purchase). They seem as much about showing off the animation's own frenetic imagistic dynamism for its own gripping sake as about encouraging LEGO consumption out in the world beyond the movie theater.

Yet maybe in its own way, the film's narration of LEGO minifigs (and, ultimately, of live-action humans playing with the minifigs) means that even when we're not directly buying (or buying into) any one LEGO product (the brick, say), we still are letting LEGO into our world (and entering into its world). The movie's speed, the general cultivation of intense viewing, whether by ramping up the on-screen display of part numbers or promoting them across quasi-trade websites or among Adult Fans of LEGO, all contribute to an image-intensity that can be repurposed as part of a promotional surround that may help drive the less-committed viewer's conviction that these movies have been comprehensively thought through. Indeed, one marketing expert, Andrew Essex, in his volume *The End of Advertising*, centrally cites *The LEGO Movie* as a key example of the expansive direction (selling a branded world that envelops a product more than just the particularized product itself) he feels advertising needs to take in order to remain effective: in Essex's words, "a brand can simply do *nothing*, and choose the dignified and much appreciated idea of sponsoring another quality story without commercial interruption."[2]

Maybe it's a fundamental economic irony of *The LEGO Movie* that it serves clearly as a tie-in to the toy, but doesn't seem to be much interested in direct promotion and is more concerned with offering its own irreducibly dynamic cinematic experience. (The irony could then, as Andrew Essex suggests, include the paradox of a film that seems to avoid direct salesmanship while giving narrative form to the building of the brand.)

It is inviting, perhaps, to imagine with the diverse tie-ins of a multimedia franchise that each branch will perform the same salesmanship as every other. From the 1990s on, The LEGO Group had itself been tempted by the cross-marketing promises of the digital and of moving-image narrative. As two business consultants, Majken Schultz and Mary Jo Hatch, commissioned to advise the company on branding, described LEGO ventures as they found them in 2003, "They [TLG] introduced new digital toys (e.g., LEGO MINDSTORMS™, LEGO SPYBOTICS™) and created virtual communities to support users and cross-sell to them (lego.com). They formed new business units, including LEGO Interactive (computer-based play materials) and LEGO Direct (catalogue sales)."[3] TV series, webcasts, and films, both short and long, were also part of the synergy.

Yet the company knew it had to maintain traditional (hence, physical) toy play as its core business: as David Robertson notes in his business history of the company, the 2000s saw TLG re-trenching around the idea of the brick. There were limits to media convergence—and at some level there always have to be. To the extent that convergence assumes at the extreme a merging of diverse media into one platform as a single and singular experience, it is belied by the very particularity of each media form, never totally reducible to neighbors it might be complementary with (but never identical to).

Quite obviously, a physical LEGO figure simply is not played with in the same way that a LEGO movie is watched. Indeed, one recommendation of Schultz and Hatch, the business consultants, as the twenty-first century began, was that TLG implement a set of directly divergent yet parallel goals for the company, each offering a different "portal" (their word) to the overall LEGO experience–each, it was hoped, providing its own path, however metaphoric, in support of the original philosophy of play organized around brick-building:

Four categories of consumer experience were defined by analysis of the things consumers do with LEGO play materials:

- EXPLORE, where young children explore themselves and the world around them through play;

- MAKE & CREATE, where consumers engage in construction and building processes creating their own universe (this category was a revitalization of the classic and neglected LEGO creative construction);

- STORIES & ACTION, where consumers involve themselves in predefined stories, characters, or universes (e.g., Star Wars, Harry Potter, Jack Stone[4]); and

- NEXT, where consumers find the most innovative construction play materials that go considerably beyond the brick, e.g., LEGO® Studios (movies/ music), MINDSTORMS (robotics), and SPYBOTICS (minirobots).[5]

For our purposes, the distinction drawn between MAKE & CREATE play and STORIES & ACTION consumption is particularly salient. There was recognition here by TLG that construction and narration each have their own valences and their own ways of inviting in a fan base. For example, as Schultz and Hatch clarify, "The new strategy positioned LEGO products within categories of consumer experience, with classic LEGO construction sets and attendant minifigures framed as the means to 'Make & Create,' while Star Wars, Harry Potter, and other licensed sets became a path to 'Stories & Action.'"[6] There is divergence here as much as convergence, as one entertainment company seeks multiple ways to engage consumers across multiple platforms, both physical and virtual. You play with LEGO; you watch a movie.

There is, on the one hand, for instance, the physical LEGO brick. It's simultaneously striking and unassuming in its stark simplicity as you grasp it, turning the rectangle around in your hand and then clicking other pieces onto it. The simple form holds vast creative possibilities: as many of the books devoted to LEGO wax on at length, combine the first brick with even a very few others and you've got mathematically expansive permutations to play with.

On the other hand, there are the TV shows and movies. By proxy, you can hold them, if you wish, in your hand (for example, by means of an iPhone or iPad, but then it's really the material support that you then manipulate). This support also typically takes the form of a rectangle—the screen format (one that is elongated in the case of *The LEGO Movie*, digitally crafted to look like widescreen cinema)—but rendered now as a container for preconstituted adventures that transpire within its borders.

While LEGO originated with the notion of creative, self-determined play—and while new media claim to be all about finding "interactivity"—the only direct interaction a spectator can have with the film is a relatively passive one. (Two adult friends of mine to whom I recommended the movie found it hard to watch, because of what they both saw as the relentlessness of its chase sequences.) And it's not just because that rush of images turns the spectator into a consumer of the speedy spectacle. As noted above, there are deliberate, key moments to the film where the image torrent slows down—dialogue and expository sequences, moments of extended slo-mo, instances of deep reflection—yet these are also viewed passively; true, loads of "Easter Eggs" might be a reason for a viewer to try to control the pace of image flow (for example, a freeze frame can reveal a poster with a translation of the Russian title for *21 Jump Street*, "Macho and the Nerd," on the wall of Emmet's apartment), but just letting those images flow over and through oneself seems the more likely way to experience the inexorable narrative movement of this screen entertainment.

Of course, virtually by definition, movies are about the unrelenting flow of images past the spectator. But the intensity of that can vary (through dynamics of pacing, amount of information packed into each image, and so on) and, as well, can be interrupted or toyed with (through, for instance, cutaways, critical commentary, pauses, and so forth). *The LEGO Movie* distinguishes itself—and this stands as another way the film holds together its tensions—by its simultaneous ability to deliver on standard action tropes (it has *lots* of forward motion in its chase sequences, putting us directly and uncritically into its kinetic thrust) *and* to step back from sheer kinesis by means of self-aware critical analysis (for example, the speechifying, which puts all heroic action into question).

Of course, like so many other recent films of action—especially ones, like *The LEGO Movie*, with their animation shot in 3D with the obvious hope of exploiting the excitement of

explosions of motion into and out of the screen, often in virtual independence from narrative and from depicted content
(dynamism, then, for its own sake)—*The LEGO Movie* is from
its very first shot (a tipping down of the credit background to
become a horizontal plane of LEGO extending into the distance) often "about" a breathless rush forward, the digital animation mimicking a camera zooming through space so that
scenic elements pass by it into the offscreen foreground. Like
other 3D, *The LEGO Movie* predictably sets out to show off the
effect whenever it can: things assail the camera (for example,
we get to look up at LEGO "water" coming down when Emmet
takes a shower), and characters and vehicles and the camera
with them are endlessly zooming toward the background
or foreground.[7] Even before the narrative gets going, and is
revealed to often be centered itself on chases through space
(thereby giving a bit of motivation to dynamic movement),
the film announces motion itself, relatively independent of
the specifics of story, as a source of fascination in its own right.

Beyond story, beyond meaning, *The LEGO Movie* offers the
visual, virtual experience of watching the building and unbuilding of a world of toys. And here it matters that the film is about
LEGO: it's not so much that solid characters rush through
solid spaces, but that, for all the seeming solidity, *everything* in the LEGO universe can be dismantled—violently torn
apart and reduced to mere elements, back to the brick. This
occurs at three levels: the environments the minifigs move
through, the props (vehicles especially, but also costumes,
weapons, and so on) they have at their disposal, and also the
minifigs themselves as beings built up from a fundamental
core of plastic elements to which appendages are added. At

the broadest level, the film whizzes through an array of sites and venues that we see the rapid assembly of but also the breaking apart of. Here there is an interesting in-joke referring to the fact that Emmet is a construction worker (but one who builds new spaces by breaking down others), since that line of work was one of the first to be incorporated by the LEGO company in its earliest sets. (Another recurrent occupation for LEGO minifigs, referenced by Good Cop/Bad Cop in the movie, is the policeman—whose original LEGO function, it would seem, was to ensure the regulation of the urban work flow).[8] By not simply creating an identity-less building block toy (the anonymous brick) but by, with the invention of the minifig, offering specialized pieces that can be assembled together to fashion characters with defined identities and defined jobs, the construction worker above all, the LEGO company makes toys that, we might say, allegorize the process of construction: one builds LEGO worlds that include builders who can, it would be imagined, be themselves building up worlds.

The forward rush of the camera simulation that opens *The LEGO Movie*, and that serves as a constant visual motif throughout this film that is so much about quest and chase, traverses large-scale constructions. These often are shown coming apart as the camera assails them, as when, during a pursuit through the city by Bad Cop, Emmet cries to Wyldstyle, "I want to go home," and the camera crashes us through a LEGO home that comes flying apart while Emmet laments, "That's not what I meant!" (In a nice in-joke, the house resembles that of the Simpsons from the FOX TV series.) Smashing through environments can also entail leaving behind whatever current LEGO world one is in, as several times the crash

Creative destruction

through brick walls and barriers leads one either into another LEGO world (the fall, for instance, into the Old West) or into a Void, a space beyond LEGO space (which we learn, in the film's big twist, is the human world, a basement filled with LEGO constructions).

In their frenetic rush through environments in *The LEGO Movie*, the LEGO figures engage with LEGO props, vehicles especially, but these often are as unstable, as open to recrafting, as the seemingly solid decors that keep coming apart. LEGO brick sets initially included fully fabricated vehicles (little metal cars, for instance) but, bit by bit, the scaling down of the minifigs into their small size enabled vehicles that were themselves brick-built and could contain minifigs within them. In *The LEGO Movie*, we are introduced first to a mass of cars, all resembling each other, proceeding in lock-step through a morning rush hour energized by the "Everything Is Awesome" song. This is the movement, we might say, of fixity: the cars flow in determined patterns through space and maintain shape as they do so. But the automatized movement of the cars in rhythm gives way soon to more chaotic, more destructive vehicular movement as Wyldstyle rescues Emmet from Good Cop/Bad Cop and a swervy, smashy chase through the city ensues. Now, it's not just environments that are built up and knocked down (for example, the violently broken-up Simpson house), but vehicles which keep being dismantled and re-formed as the chase ensues. From this point on, there will be lots of diverse vehicles, often ones cobbled together, rather than just the similarly shaped and simplified cars everyone in Bricksburg seems predictably to have owned, and these later vehicles will transform to be recrafted to new environments, new necessities. (Land vehicles, for instance, can become aquatic or otherwise when need be; at one point, on the fly, Batman converts an aerial vehicle Bad Cop is in into a baby carriage and the perambulator comes tumbling down.) It's noteworthy that at several points, right in the middle of a chase, the pursuer or the pursued rebuild their vehicles in the moment, not slowing down, but grabbing whatever LEGO pieces at hand fit the transformation. Often, as noted, as the character improvises their new vehicle by scanning around for the necessary parts, we see on the screen the actual LEGO number for that part (and a random check suggests that, indeed, this numbering is accurate), as if enumerating pieces that could be useful to this or that project in the real world, including buying and building vehicles like the ones in the movie. But just as other montages of LEGO transformation don't seem to be directly about salesmanship, the parts numbers flash by too quickly to be very useful to us: it's more likely that, as we see with other aspects of *The LEGO Movie* as a potential tie-in to the physical, purchasable LEGO toys, the ultimate goal is not direct salesmanship (it is unclear that these

A constructed, catalogued world

numbers flitting by would lead us to buy those pieces) but
overall immersion in the brand of all things (and all experiences) LEGO.[9]

Falling into Narrative

Of course, *The LEGO Movie* is more than endless dynamics and endless transformation. The energetic movement that introduces the film's first sequence does come to an end, seeming almost to bump up against seer Vitruvius and cutting swiftly on the same axis to a closer shot in which he portentously announces, "He is coming"—the prophecy, that is, that a special figure will eventually appear to challenge attempts to fix the LEGO world in place. The first swift camera movement transitions into story-telling, then, but only after signaling that the film has other experiences to offer than narrative dramatics alone.

And in any case, the film seems at the outset deliberately unclear as to what sort of story it wants to tell—the serious quest of a hero figure, the comic tale of LEGO toys playing (and being played) at being heroes, or some sort of transformative and intentionally insecure mix of options such as these? Vitruvius's sententious prophecy is immediately followed by his warning, "Cover your butt." If the opening movement had announced the film's ongoing concern with dynamics for their own sake, somewhat divorced from narrative demands, the butt admonition undercuts the solemnity of this first important narrative pronouncement through arch silliness of expression (and the film compounds the jokiness by having an assistant query "cover your what?"). Even as it falls from sheer visual spectacle into story, *The LEGO Movie* confirms that it won't take story too seriously—that humorous deflation will be its dominant take on any too-tempting hint of profundity and meaningfulness.

In addition, any sententiousness in Vitruvius's first phrase is further qualified by our recognition that the very prophesizing of a Special Savior by an African American (followed just a few scenes later by the supportive efforts of a kickass woman heroine in black) is an obvious reference to *The Matrix*. As action movie in the vein of mythic heroic quest, *The LEGO Movie* doesn't stand alone but acknowledges the popular culture around it and that it is often in explicit debt to.

Just as *The Matrix* had Laurence Fishburne serve as mentor to its yet-to-be-fully-realized protagonist so as to bring out his special talents, so does *The LEGO Movie* rely on an African American actor to play the wizened figure of spiritual inspiration (what some, such as Spike Lee, have termed "the magical Negro," the figure who has no life of his [less often, her] own and exists simply to enable white heroes to realize the best of themselves). Morgan Freeman has seemingly made a career of playing such figures, to the degree that his appearance in such a role has become a convention that can be played upon.[1]

The filmmakers are indeed aware of movie tropes such as these. Thus, the DVD for *The LEGO Movie* includes a hilarious promotional clip of line readings by the main minifigs to LEGO versions of directors Phil Lord and Chris Miller. When they get to Vitruvius, he can't find his place in the script, so Lord Business, dictatorially taking over from Lord and Miller, directs him to say "something about the fate of the world," as if acknowledging that that's what Morgan Freeman does inevitably and portentously in so many films.

Who's really in charge here?

The ironic stance of *The LEGO Movie* itself does much to undercut the racial politics of the African-American-as-sage-to-white-people, while cannily persisting in the convention even as it's played with. As some commentators have noted, the helper figure of the spiritualized African American sage often involves a neutering of the character, who not only in general has no life of his/her own but specifically has no *sexual or romantic* life: his or her function is to enable romance between white leads and then, often, to step back. (The extreme example might be *The Legend of Bagger Vance* [2000], where in a 1930s South that seems pretty bereft of racism, the task of the black man [Will Smith] is to bring the two white stars—Matt Damon and Charlize Theron—together in a kiss and then walk off into the sunset, waving back as he disappears into legend.)

Of course, as a PG animated film, *The LEGO Movie* might well be expected to shy away from any overt sexuality, black *or* white. (There was evidently a scene where Lord Business's revealingly named "Micro-managers," supposedly scouring the bottom of the ocean to find an escaped Emmet, were discovered actually to be making out with mermaids, but that was cut, as was a moment where Emmet and Wyldstyle kiss. Evidently, parents at preview screenings objected that such amorous activity was not appropriate in a LEGO movie, and the scenes were removed.)[2] At the same time, though, we might notice in recent works of animation and in other superhero narratives, whether animated or live-action, a creeping up of more adult moments, even as the putative audience is often imagined to be kids. PG in rating, *The LEGO Movie* stands alongside R-rated superhero fare like *Deadpool*, and it is clear (as anyone who's gone to see *Deadpool* at a movie theater and witnessed general nonconformity by exhibitors with adhering to the over-17 rule) that the films exist in a continuum, rather than in silos coded by age. Indeed, like other works of PG animation, *The LEGO Movie* sometimes sublimates edginess around sexuality into a somewhat related edginess around body function (it includes flatulence jokes along with "butt" jokes) and corporeal crudeness (its PG rating is, in the wonderful telegraphic style of the rating system, said to be due to "Mild Action and Rude Humor"). At the same time, for all its endearing lightness in key moments (as in the sweet and innocent, even sugary world of Cloud Cuckooland where everything is bright and cheerful), *The LEGO Movie* does appear to target viewers beyond the youngest kids through the subplot of Wyldstyle's relationship with boyfriend Batman: here, there is discussion of what it means to be an amorous couple in a manner that, while not sexualized, is certainly more adolescent or adult than child-like.

Indeed, the neutering of African-Americanness through the "Magical Negro" trope perhaps has as its converse corollary Batman's obsession in the film with blackness/darkness as emblematic of brooding masculinity. Just as, in *The Matrix*, protagonists (and eventual amorous partners) Trinity and Neo, taught well by mentor Morpheus (Fishburne), don sleek dark coats to signify coolness as they attack the enemy's skyscraper fortress, so too do Batman and Wyldstyle adopt a dark Goth look that gives them a broody edginess absent elsewhere in the film. For what it's worth, Wyldstyle doesn't stay in that mode, revealing that beneath her tough punkiness there resides sweet and nice Lucy. On the other hand, Batman stays tough to the end and, maybe as a reward for his edgy spirit, gets his own spin-off LEGO movie.

In capaciously and capriciously pulling in existing conventions whenever it can and commenting explicitly on them, *The LEGO Movie* isn't offering a stand-alone fiction of its own, somehow assumed to exist in and of itself, but a deliberately derivative experience, filled with allusion and reference. The narrative shows itself to be an enthusiastic assemblage of known and accepted motifs and scenes and premises from across the history of modern popular culture (and it relies on our sharing in this, as when Emmet, taken into custody early on and interrogated by a surly cop [voiced by Liam Neeson], insists that his knowledge of television shows makes him certain that every bad cop must be accompanied by a good one). The allusive nature of *The LEGO Movie* again cautions against interpretation: scenes are assembled not for their unique and independent meanings but for their representativeness and stereotypicality, allowing jokes to be made at their own admitted conventionality and enabling new twists on the conventions. To take just one example, when a camera movement surges outward from the mass of construction activities in what seems to be a typical day at work for Emmet, a surveillance camera comes into view as the space expands: to say that we "interpret" this as a

sign of surveillance society would seem to exceed the deliberate obviousness of the visual gesture, the clarity with which
the film establishes the motif. (And we recognize the moment
because we are all aware, from politics *and* popular culture,
what surveillance society looks like.)

If the visual dynamics work against meaning, so too does
the narrative itself. From the hero quest that undergirds the
narrative to the discussions of relationship to the depiction of
corporate power, *The LEGO Movie* traffics cleverly with the
already known—with motifs and meanings the viewer has already experienced in popular culture at large and therefore
watches now for their commonality and conventionality, and
for what can be done to them playfully, rather than for a stand-
alone purity of purpose and a uniqueness of insight.

Nowhere is the play of irony more evident than in those
moments where *The LEGO Movie* recognizes and accepts the
very potential of mass art, including itself as a work of popular
culture, to overwhelm us and distract us from any critical position, including political ones: thus, when President Business
admits openly on television that his plan is to put everyone to
sleep, Emmet perks up with concern only to have any wor-
ries allayed when the television programming immediately
switches to an advertisement for the mind-draining hit TV
show *Where Are My Pants?*, which, as far as we can see, offers
nothing but a husband endlessly intoning that phrase as he
scrambles to get ready for work. The scene can bring to mind a
similar one in François Truffaut's 1966 dystopian adaptation of
Fahrenheit 451, wherein protagonist Montag's wife and some
of her invited guests watch on a wrap-around screen banal
situations that render viewers mindless. These are savage critiques of the deliberately numbing effects of the products of

the Culture Industry, but where *Fahrenheit 451* can claim that
its Art Cinema background raises it above the seemingly empty
fare of television (often a foil to the art of cinema, imagined
as superior culture), *The LEGO Movie*—as animation, as toy
derivative, as assemblage of preexisting tropes and conventions of popular culture, as spectacle-filled diversion in its own
right—is implicated in the very forms of escapism it assails. It
is ultimately on a pop cultural continuum with *Where Are My
Pants?*, even as it mocks the TV show. (Interestingly, the last
live-action segment of *The LEGO Movie 2*—wherein Finn and
his sister Bianca, under the approving eyes of their mother,
reconcile the worlds of LEGO and DUPLO so that everything
seems to be happily ever after—concludes with the offscreen
voice of the father imploring, "Honey, where are my pants?," in
a sly aside that implicates humans in the banality of everyday
life such as we witnessed in conformist Bricksburg in the first
film).[3]

The LEGO Movie's avowed *ironic and yet fully accepting*
participation in the Culture Industry becomes all the more
pronounced when Emmet leaves for work in his car and
switches on the top pop song, "Everything Is Awesome"—a hit
not only in Bricksburg within the film's fiction, but for the
world at large that greeted *The LEGO Movie* in 2014. (As noted
earlier, it was an Academy Award nominee for Best Song.)
Cheesy bubble-gum pop with a relentlessly driving and cy-
clical beat, "Everything Is Awesome" became ubiquitous in
2014, especially for kids (who made the word "Awesome" even
more ubiquitous than it had been hitherto). It combines grat-
ing repetitiveness with a catchiness that is hard to shake off.
(On the directors' commentary track for the DVD, they offer
self-aware apologies to America for all the damage the song

did!) As pop, "Everything Is Awesome" itself embodies key contradictions of mass entertainment: its very banality of form,
its sheer kitsch quality, makes it lovable and inescapable (*as
well as unbearable*), even as its first iteration in the film is held
up for criticism for its very inescapability. Former Devo co-
founder and lead singer Mark Mothersbaugh—who had experience with animation, having served as composer for the
Rugrats television show and movies—produced the film's version of the song (as well as arranging the film's music overall),
written by Shawn Patterson, JoLi, and The Lonely Island. In
an interview with FOX News, Mothersbaugh admitted the
cloying complicity of the song: "[It] was supposed to be like
mind control early in the film. It's totally irritating, this kind
of mindless mantra to get people up and working. It's like the
whip crack on their back."[4] Indeed, the first iteration of the song
is all about unthinking conformity: Emmet joins in a stream
of fellow workers all in their same-model cars, distinguished
only by the pseudo-individualization of differences in color,
going blithely to work (and passing a billboard that advertises
"One Car: Some Variety") and then proceeding to their tasks
with bouncy alacrity. The sequence is affective and effective
in its fast cutting with sweeping simulations of dynamic camera movement, all keyed to the veritably robot-like gestures
of the LEGO energetically laboring away. We, complacent
viewers lined up in our movie seats, watch this overpowering
spectacle of rhythm and subordinated labor as our own critical values are played with by a synthesis of sound and visual
kinesis that sets itself up as inescapably overwhelming. Potentially, we are as beaten into submission by pop culture as
the characters themselves, and the film seems to relish that
possibility.[5]

The pop rhythm of conformity

Yet the twists go even farther. Maybe bad music is in its own way good: who knows? Indeed, as Mark Mothersbaugh himself goes on to declare of "Everything Is Awesome" in his interview with FOX, "By the end of the movie . . . instead of being just a mindless, go-to-work song, it becomes about co-operation and people working together to do bigger things."

The acceptance of gluey pop as a means for people to grow together rather than be enslaved together becomes even more pronounced in *The LEGO Movie 2*, which offers by its end a full endorsement of itself as a utopian musical in which the supposedly positive reconciliatory qualities of music are celebrated. To be sure, early in this follow-up film, when we see Bricksburg turned into a derelict space of every-person-for-himself savagery, where all cheerfulness has been banished (except for that experienced by ever-optimistic but also ever-clueless Emmet), Emmet can only listen to "Everything Is Awesome" privately, as a track heard through headphones on his personal music device. The song neither serves the function of bringing all citizens into robotic regularity, as it did early on in the first LEGO feature, nor yet hints at any affirmative possibilities of music as *group* celebration. Indeed,

when key LEGO figures leave Bricksburg (either spirited away
by the DUPLO or going off to rescue the kidnapped brethren),
their encounters with new worlds populated by new sorts of
characters, *ones who embrace musicality*, are initially deemed
by the familiar LEGO characters—Lucy especially—to be sus-
picious and foreboding, as if the collective embrace of music
equates to collective enslavement. For instance, when Emmet
and his team travel through outer space in an attempt to save
Wyldstyle and the others, they first encounter a sunny planet
overrun with bouncy musicality where everything conspires to
portend mindless enslavement—a bright, candy-colored suburbia where everyone dances to the same cloying beat. The
scene evokes and invokes a tradition of paranoid nightmares
of average everyday life where everyone has become zombi-
fied (from Shirley Jackson's "The Lottery," to the identical tract
houses where kids bounce balls in lifeless unison in Madeleine
L'Engle's *A Wrinkle in Time*, to the animatronic pseudo-life
of housewives in *The Stepford Wives*, to the buoyant repetitiveness of "Good morning! And in case I don't see you, good
afternoon, good evening, and good night!" in *The Truman
Show*) and where the very unquestioning cheerfulness of suburbia or small-town America is itself the sign of enslavement.

Yet what at first seems frightening and foreboding—the up-
tempo ditty "This song's gonna get stuck inside your head"—
turns out by the sequel's end to be a positive force: music's
contagion, the film ultimately asserts, is wonderful and brings
unity and love out from conflict. It's worth noting that one iteration of "Everything Is Awesome" in the sequel is a downbeat/
minor-key version, sung wistfully at one point by Wyldstyle—
an act that importantly allows Emmet to start suspecting

another, mellower, side to her seeming Goth identity. The final irony of *The LEGO Movie 2*, then, after all the ironies of the first film, is to propose, ultimately, an honesty and authenticity beyond irony—and to associate this with the visceral infectiousness of pop music.

The Extraordinary Ordinariness of LEGO

Across its history, The LEGO Group has had to deal with a series of potentially incompatible goals in its cultivation of play, and both *The LEGO Movie* and its sequel offer fantasy solutions to some of these. The value, positive or negative, of pop music is just one such example.

To take another, box sets, especially the ones licensed from movie franchises, have had to find a balance, as we've noted, between enabling open-ended creative play and giving the movie fans the promise (incarnated in rule-bound instructions) that following the plan will lead to constructions that emulate iconic scenes and structures from those films. As David C. Robinson recounts in his aforementioned business history of LEGO, *Brick by Brick*, once licensing arrangements with the movies began (starting with *Star Wars* in 1999), LEGO play increasingly seemed to be more about what Robertson terms "figure-based play," where one builds preplanned models to evoke established universes inhabited by canonic figures like Star Wars or Ninjago (the latter a franchise internal to TLG, rather than a licensing), than "construction-based play," where one randomly puts together pieces that have no instructions or top-down plans behind them.

Intervening in its own narrative manner in the tensions between free play and instruction, *The LEGO Movie* initially shows disdain for slavishly following instructions, only to end by admitting that instructions sometimes really are necessary if one wants/needs to reach a defined goal.[1] Ultimately rejecting fully open-ended free play, *The LEGO Movie* assumes that every piece has its purpose and that every invention, no matter how seemingly crazy, has its fundamental function (such as Emmet's infamous double-decker couch, which everyone dismisses until they see the unexpected function it was meant to fulfill). One premise the film admits and accepts has to do with the assumption that the only thing that can stop the Kragle (the Krazy Glue, that is) from fixing the LEGO world in place is the venerated plastic element, the Piece of Resistance that gets fused early on to Emmet's back and that he is never free of until the moment he actually is able to use it to reseal the Kragle: while there are all sorts of deviations in the plot and all sorts of improvisatory moments where this or that component of the LEGO world is unbuilt and rebuilt to adapt to changed narrative obstacles, there is no deviation from the premise that the Kragle needs to be stopped and that the Piece of Resistance, remaining with Emmet through all the detours of narrative, *is* the necessary and inevitable and unique tool for that purpose. (The "Piece" is an obvious but hilarious pun on the French "pièce de resistance," and picks up astutely on that term's notion of the key element to an assemblage but also on the idea of "resistance" to power, so central to this movie.)

Emmet had ended his seemingly typical workday governed by cheerful, unquestioning, instruction-following conformity by moving away from all that: distracted, he deviates from the crowd and goes down the rabbit hole of adventure. Aptly, Lord Business's world, the world that Emmet is thrown out of, is all about omnipresent stratified work—a security force, a culture industry geared to rendering people mindless, minions and micro-managers, data processors and information gatherers, and so on, and the blue-collar workers who endlessly expand the city. When Emmet tumbles through the void at the bottom of the construction site, he also falls away from the world of labor as servitude (pointedly, his exit from this world happens when he goes in the wrong direction and leaves the crowd of fellow laborers). The contracted employee directly becomes independent: from now on, Emmet is less a worker than an adventurer, increasingly striking out on his own, and increasingly encountering worlds that seem to run by principles other than the idea of servitude. In the sequel, attractive alternatives to the business world are the benevolent feudalism on Queen Whatevra's planet and the endless self-sustaining dance energy of suburbia on the planet that Emmet and Rex arrive at. Throughout these movements away from the early image of the world of robotic labor, music persists—and even builds in importance—as the force (the glue, we might say) that unites characters in positive fashion and offers something other than mere worker obedience. Underground resistance movements, like the one the Master Builders foment, certainly have work-like obligations (they can't just hang around partying in Cloud Cuckooland while the threat of the Kragle looms over them), but their "labor" is born of dreams of freedom and self-determination, not subservience to a higher master (instead, the so-named Master Builders strive to be their own bosses of their lives, even as they seek guidance from seeming prophets like Emmet).

The reassuring fantasies—each of them an attempt to find a path between contradictions—that following instructions is a way to maintain inventiveness, that music can collectivize without fostering conformity, that adventurous efforts can put one outside the circuits of work and cycles of urban existence, and so on, connect, then, to another such fantasy: that each of us can be special—even as it's clear that for *every*one to be special maybe robs the concept of its distinction. Emmet is both the LEGO piece as anonymous element like every other, *and* the special hero of this narrative saga. The conceit of *The LEGO Movie* is the idea of the minifig as blank slate—Emmet as a regularized, generic nobody in a regularized, generic world—but the narrative then recounts how he becomes special because in a way he's always been special (just as we all have been).

In body and appendages, Emmet seems very much like most every other inhabitant of Bricksburg, and that similarity seems in keeping with the generic nature of the basic LEGO minifig: a squat round body and head, articulable limb joints with clasps at the end of the arms. Why then does Emmet—or anybody—become "special" other than through the convention that a saga needs a hero?

To be sure, as LEGO developed themed sets (for example, pirates and knights and space voyagers), minifigs were crafted with specific identities built into them (for example, an eye-patch on a pirate), and this individualizing of the generic minifig intensified with licensing of iconic characters from iconic narratives: for example, Batman is not just an individualized head that snaps onto any body whatsoever but is constituted by an entire customization from head to body to appendages to clothes, and to props that are all crafted for this specific character. The challenge, though, that *The LEGO Movie* accepted from its very inception was to make figures like Batman secondary in the narrative (even if he sometimes steals the show) and to test what kind of narrative could be built from unassuming anonymity.

And within the fictional premises of the story world, along with Emmet, most of the inhabitants of Bricksburg are indeed rendered as pretty regularized and pretty much all alike: when, as per the instruction manual for a perfect daily life that he and other denizens of the city follow slavishly, Emmet begins his awesome day by greeting the world from his balcony, we see everyone else in the city doing the same thing. This is indeed a world of uniformity and conformity, and it refers back to the LEGO brick and LEGO figurine pieces (torso, head, appendages) as a generic fount of sameness. Of course, LEGO anonymity can always be belied by creative construction: there is probably no LEGO figure less generic than the pirate Metal Beard of *The LEGO Movie*, who has been cobbled together with random parts to end up (though it's an unending end, since he seems to keep mutating further) as a sign and site of pure (or maybe impure), wacky, and garish self-refashioning.

But certainly at first, everyone in Bricksburg, including Emmet, does seem pretty much alike. It's implied, for example, that they've all been submitted to the same numbing, conforming pressures of the mass culture industry—not just by a cloying song like the overbearingly rhythmic "Everything Is Awesome" and the inane meagerness of the television show "Where Are My Pants?," but by all of everyday life, from the abodes they inhabit to the cars they drive to the mass-produced food they eat (everyone in Bricksburg seems to live for President Business's Taco Tuesdays). Like everyone else, Emmet

takes his place in lines (the stream of cars in the daily com-
mute, the queues for the dry cleaner and at the coffee shop),
and he seems absorbed fully into the standardized ordinariness of the mass (following instructions on how to live out
one's conformist morning, Emmet compliments everyone on
looking nice and gets the exact same compliment back, a further mark of his unmarked, undifferentiated nature but also
of everyone else's). Emmet is like everyone else, and they're all
pretty much like him.

Obviously, it is the point of the narrative to give Emmet
identity by offering him a mission that brings out the positive:
his ability to assume the mantle of heroism and step up in the
fight against blind and bland conformity. Yet his divergence
from mass society reveals also some negative qualities beyond
sheer clumsiness. For example, when he is under interroga-
tion and says that his neighbors and workmates can vouch
for him, the testimony video that Bad Cop unveils in response
has them, one by one, saying that they don't know much about
Emmet and that he doesn't have anything special to make him
stand out (this despite the fact that all the workers in their
cars, on lines here or there, greeting each other with the same
indoctrinated cheerfulness, and so on, all seem to have very little that makes them stand out either). Several coworkers and
neighbors and local merchants attest that Emmet is lacking in
the positive distinguishing characteristics that give individuality to other members of the Bricksburg community (such as
the sausages that one worker likes, or the beard that another
one sports). These supposedly personalizing traits—a LEGO
prop sausage in the former case, a few marks painted onto
the generic minifig face in the latter—stand as meager forms
of differentiation indeed (does liking sausage really give us

stand-out identity in anonymous, mass society?), especially within the context of the monotone, robotic regularity of Bricksburg overall. They seem an ironic comment on LEGO construction: with a few generic pieces, you can create variety by the mere snap of a prop (like a little plastic sausage), but it is always a bounded one, and it is always a question as to how far any change or addition really shakes things up and adds individuality to the overall sameness. (Later, the film makes the same point through the character of Good Cop/Bad Cop: all that has to happen is for his LEGO face to swivel around and an entire change of personality ensues, even though it's still Liam Neeson.)

The LEGO Movie, again, embraces its own contradictions here. Nongeneric characters like Batman or Wyldstyle or the highly individualized Master Builders we encounter later on in the film (with some expressed confusion between the Michelangelo of the Teenage Mutant Ninja Turtles and the Michelangelo of classical art) serve only as secondary—help-mates or advisers—to the intensely generic Emmet. They are individuals, but for this film they are not what heroes are made of. (When, in *The LEGO Movie 2*, rogue adventurer Rex declares he lionizes Emmet for his legendary exploits from the first movie, Rex explains that he sports a sleeveless vest in order to emulate Emmet's construction worker garb. The comment is a wry allusion to the omnipresence, noted earlier, of the anonymous builder figurine in LEGO history: Rex, a globe-trotting adventurer in the mode of Indiana Jones, claims to take as his model one of the most common minifigs with one of the most common jobs in mass society.)

In centering their first feature film on the generic Emmet, Warner and The LEGO Group took on the challenge of fashioning a narrative around a character who not merely has no backstory within the fictional world within the film (we never know anything about Emmet's past, whereas we are even introduced to the Good Cop/Bad Cop's parents and see their home—which we learn is outside the big city) but also derives from no previous narratives in the LEGO universe. That is, Emmet does not descend from either a licensed story world (unlike, say, Batman, who of course stars in the second LEGO feature) or a LEGO-created story world of its own with established conventions (for example, Ninjago, a television series as well as the source for a LEGO feature spin-off).

In assuming this challenge, the filmmakers astutely return to the fundamental philosophy of LEGO system building—you start with anonymous pieces but can craft them into something unique—and make it the premise for story-building. Of course, there are unique characters created for the film that seem to have little of Emmet's generic quality: on the one hand, Vitruvius, Lord Business, and Wyldstyle, among others, do not preexist the movie and in that respect are similar to Emmet; on the other hand, they have individualized looks that give them identity (and, with Wyldstyle, we even get a bit of backstory, including the insecurities that have led her to make constant name changes). In contrast, Emmet is little more than a generic placeholder—the average city builder, like so many such builders across LEGO history. To give such a character the potential to have a narrative centered on him, the film assembles themes and iconic situations and motifs from across the field of modern popular culture and plunks Emmet into them (while fully admitting it is doing so): the story Emmet drops into (literally so, when he plunges through a gap in the construction site) is built out of modern mythologies from mass

Accident of fate?

culture, such as the recurrent trope of the quest and ultimate
battle with ultimate evil.

But to the extent that the fall into story *The LEGO Movie*
enacts when Emmet departs his uneventful, essentially non-
narrative way of being (where "Everything Is Awesome," but
nothing ever seems to change) takes him dramatically into a
world of pursuit, battle, menace, and so on, *The LEGO Movie*
then has to negotiate another tension running through the
history of LEGO and the company behind the toy. For decades, the philosophy of LEGO centered essentially on what
we might term nonnarrativized and especially nonconflictual
play: that is, building and unbuilding wasn't so much about
following a story—and certainly not about setting up violent
fights between opposing forces—as about randomly making
and taking apart. But as LEGO increasingly emphasized, by
the late 1970s and early 1980s, themed sets—its pirates, castles, and outer-space lines, for example—and then pegged
these to licensing around intellectual property that was itself
narrative in form (specifically, sets based on fiction films and
television stories, so that, for instance, outer space became less
generic and turned into the outer space of Star Wars), story

became omnipresent and brought with it realms of action and struggle against opponents in a manner that could seem at odds with a philosophy of play as nonconflictual. For instance, where once TLG had refused to include weapons among the props (even for the ubiquitous policemen), these now became requisite to the violent encounters that came with action narrative. And when the company would pull back from modern depictions of real-world violence, it found that fans were only too happy to craft their own weaponized minifigs as part of the end-user phenomenon known as MOC (My Own Creation).

Weaponized Frank Sinatra as presidential assassin from the movie Suddenly! *(courtesy of David Doll)*

True, the armaments that TLG allowed to enter its narrative worlds tended to be more the fantasy items of science fiction (lasers, light sabers, outer space cannons, and so on) than worldly weapons from our present reality, but by the 2000s LEGO was insistently giving itself over to play centered on violent action and dramatic conflict.[2] The reconciliation of father and son in *The LEGO Movie* serves, then, as a kind of pacifying truce and a conversion of goal-oriented narrative

activity back into random, open-ended play. The arrival of the
DUPLO just after this reconciliation—and just as the movie
ends—threatens the achieved harmony and brings conflictual
narrative back to the fore; it's one of the complications, then,
of *The LEGO Movie 2* that what the DUPLO ultimately offer
is to uncomplicate things through another—and higher—level
of reconciliation beyond conflict. (This adds to the mystery of
what a third film might have been about, since the second film
ends fully in harmony and happiness, and with family members in the "real" world participating willingly in the peace, so
that it is hard to imagine where conflict now could come from.)

The awesomeness of family

The communal (in this case, familial) celebration of achieved
harmony in *The LEGO Movie* and its sequel also offers a fantasy
resolution to another tension in the history of LEGO, one I
discussed earlier: the seeming contradiction between the sheer
number of people who worked on *The LEGO Movie* and its
narrative fiction's invocation of one special person who makes
all the difference (along with LEGO's guiding philosophy of
personal creativity). Quite simply, LEGO play often plays out

as a solitary activity: you take the bricks and you make what you want, but the factory manufacture of LEGO pieces and the craft production of *The LEGO Movie* are of necessity large-scale operations. True, at the consumer end of things, there have been famous group efforts in LEGO construction, especially around large-scale display at conventions and efforts at team-based record-breaking, and usually on massive creations that require lots of participants working together (bold and big LEGO ventures are a constant source for entries, and their updating, in the Guinness record books). But these require complicated attention to scale and compatibility (for example, you can't collectively build a LEGO town unless everyone agrees on the scale of the streets and so on, and unless there is compatibility between individual contributions).

The LEGO Movie disdains corporate control of creativity even as it seeks an acceptable form for collective enterprise. As it does in other respects, the film tries to imagine several forms of creativity at once: Emmet is special in coming up with the project to invade Lord Business's tower, but then every other minifig in the tight team makes his or her irreducible contribution to Emmet's special plan. Between personal inventiveness and large-scale industry (such as the vast crew behind the movie itself), *The LEGO Movie* invokes the possibility of small-team effort and imagines the work of the tight collective as a form of rebellious opposition and resistance to corporate power. Somewhat like the a movie, where a select group of professionals, each with their own specialized skills, breaks into a place to steal something (think *Ocean's Eleven*, both the original and the remake), *The LEGO Movie* portrays an assemblage of highly individualized figures (Emmet, along with Batman, Vitruvius, Wyldstyle, 80s Space Guy, Unikitty, and Metal

Beard) who break into a fortress-like locale (Lord Business's corporate skyscraper)—although in this case not for theft, but to prevent universal calamity (in this respect, it is probably as much like a group superhero franchise film, Justice League or Avengers, say, as a heist film). And like a heist film, it imagines that the work one does together with one's equally skilled but individualized coworkers is something other than anonymous labor for a big corporation. Yes, if you're trying to pull off a heist you have to report readily to work just as you would in a 9-to-5 job (time is so important to corporate work but also to the stealth work of a team worming its way in synchronicity into the infrastructure of the system), but you do so while maintaining your own unique identity tied to your own talents. *The LEGO Movie* is cheerful about noncorporate teamwork: through the sharing of skills, the members of the team avoid being absorbed back into the drone-like activities of anonymous mass labor.[3]

The film narrates how Emmet gets separated from the crowd of drone-like figurines all moving in conformist unison. But it's a separation that enables him to discover both his own individual irreducibility *and to form a small group collective with talented individuals, each with their own irreducible skill*. Conversely, as we've seen, *The LEGO Movie 2* uses pop music (the inescapable "This song's gonna get stuck inside your head") as a mark of *large-scale* recollectivization: just as an entire city moved robotically to the beat of "Everything Is Awesome" in the first *LEGO Movie*, now multiple worlds all seem to be grooving in unison to the beat. To get with the program, to fall in line with collective unity, ends up as a positive virtue. Out in the "real" world of the second film, there is still the small collectivity of brother and sister playing LEGO and

DUPLO together, but within the toy world itself, small-scale teamwork gives way to mass celebration, mass harmony.

In the first film, it takes narrative to get to collectivity, however tight-knit: in other words, there has to be a movement from the deadening collective conformity of a Bricksburg dominated by mental and manual enslavement to the enlivening harmony of family and small-scale teamwork centered on each and every one's irreducible contributions to community. One can leave Bricksburg behind, but as long as the menace of Lord Business remains, there can be no freedom and no end to the conflicts that drive narrative on. From the moment (around thirteen minutes in) that Wyldstyle liberates Emmet from Good Cop/Bad Cop and the threat of being melted down, the film becomes not merely an action movie but a pursuit story: Emmet and Wyldstyle go on the run, through the Old West, joined by Vitruvius and then Batman, along with a number of other LEGO minifigs. Batman's entry into the film no doubt aids in this transition: he makes a film about a nonhero, whom everyone is pushing to be the hero they need, into an actual superhero movie. Batman is a character who gets things done. He also, as we see with his reservations about the relentless cheerfulness of Cloud Cuckooland, brings a world-weary cynicism to the enterprise of resistance. Batman confirms the movie's move beyond anodyne urban portrait into a more vibrant genre experience.

Yet if the jumps from Bricksburg to the Old West and then to Cloud Cuckooland are sudden and dramatic, the move to these spaces away from the big city, and away from the threat of state violence if one gets out of line, allows for some stock-taking that creates veritable pauses in the narrative. Story doesn't end but takes a breather of one sort or another.

For example, after another wild chase that takes them from a cowboy saloon, Emmet, Wyldstyle, and Vitruvius leave the western setting behind to enter into the space of Emmet's mind, shown as a vast field of white LEGO with nothing around it (I'll talk about the animation of this scene later). Here, again, in this evident allusion to *The Matrix*, there is important exposition that offers a break from the chase to impart useful background (we learn that Emmet knows of the "man upstairs"). Likewise, the arrival at Cloud Cuckooland seems to bring another respite from the chase (until it's discovered that Good Cop/Bad Cop had a tracking device placed on Emmet and the chase begins again). Time initially seems suspended in Cloud Cuckooland, a place where there are no rules (and no obvious labor, just characters endlessly having fun) and where techno-music offers a beat no less unavoidable than that of "Everything Is Awesome," but that is now assumed to enable an authentic version of buoyant cheer (predictably, and astutely, Batman notes that he's going to hate the place).

Moments of respite are also occasions for discussion and debate. For instance, as Wyldstyle and Emmet ride through the Old West to meet up with Vitruvius, she takes time to explain her relationship situation (she informs Emmet she has a boyfriend—later revealed to be Batman—and that it is all "super-serious") and then to offer a long recap of how Lord Business siloed various LEGO worlds from each other. It transpires, though, that the doltish Emmet hasn't really listened to Wyldstyle's backstory explanation, so the recap doesn't even matter. In keeping with the overall strategy of comic deflation, moments where characters speak meaningfully about big issues and about their narrative mission are typically undone in one way or another. To take another example, when, at

Cloud Cuckooland, Emmet begins an impassioned but nervous speech to the Master Builders about how he relates, as an ordinary guy called up to be "Special," to the prophecy that a savior would arrive to save the day, his reservations about taking up the mantle of heroism turn all the Master Builders against him—instead of inspiring them, as we imagined he would do as reluctant hero, but hero nonetheless.

In a more consequential break in narrative progress, Emmet and Wyldstyle's meandering journey is interrupted by a cross-cut back to the city, and to Lord Business's high-rise headquarters. This is fully a world of techno-modernity as minions type away on computers, and screens and read-outs inform Business of Emmet and Wyldstyle's whereabouts and confirm the extent to which this animated film is all about a world of data collection endlessly offered up on screen devices. It's a world, too, that the real, human world of the toys' owners infiltrates, but in ways not understood by the LEGO minifigs (and perhaps by much of the real audience at this point): Lord Business shows to Good Cop/Bad Cop real-world objects that have turned up in the LEGO world (presumably they have been dropped in from the human framing world) and that remain a mystery, except for the Kragle—which a close-up of the tube reveals to be Krazy Glue, maybe providing us with our first awareness of the humans behind and beyond the film's seemingly self-contained LEGO universe. For what it's worth, there are in fact earlier hints of the human world, but they pass by quickly and probably don't add up to much for the viewer the first time around. For example, around nine minutes into the film, when Emmet touches the Piece of Resistance, he has photographic-style visions of "the man upstairs" and of a kid—later revealed to be the father and his son

Finn. More teasingly, but also more obscurely, the demolition and rebuilding instructions at the construction site where we see Emmet working are shown fleetingly to be in larger scale than the minifigs working with them, the implication being that these are the sort of plans that come with real-life LEGO sets and that have been dropped by Finn or his dad into the fictional, and smaller than human, LEGO world that Emmet and his coworkers inhabit. Since Emmet's grand, nearly successful plan will involve following the instructions (and drawing his own) in order to sneak into Lord Business's office tower, these earlier "blueprints" can signal an important part of Finn's psychological evolution as the human who presumably guides Emmet's actions. From early on in the movie, there's the dropped clue (literally dropped perhaps into Emmet's world) that Finn somewhat follows the instructions (of both TLG and his dad), but nests them inside the fictional world he's constructed within his real world so that they can seem to be his own choice and not a "relic" of the father's interdictions— those other crucial paper instructions against free play that are fastened with masking tape to the sides of the tables supporting the LEGO constructions.[4]

Strikingly, indeed, just when the narrative conflict seems to be building to its crescendo—Emmet and his gang infiltrating Lord Business's domain—*The LEGO Movie* breaks from digital animation to photographic reality in order to reveal the human world for whom these LEGO are playthings. *The LEGO Movie* seems, in this leap to the human level of existence, to hold out the promise of a real world beyond fiction, beyond fantasy. And this is a "real world" where fairly simple virtues and values get reaffirmed—a dad's love for his son, the dad's recognition that too much emotional rigidity can damage a family, the concomitant realization that personal creativity is a virtue to be cultivated, and so on. It may be worth noting that toy stories that frame the adventures of animate toys within the larger narrative of the humans who possess and play with them often imagine these frames as more real, more simple, more honest, more fundamental, than the fantasy stories within them: for example, the move to live action in a film like the 1977 *Raggedy Ann and Andy* is all about an authenticity of love, belonging, the idyll of owner and doll. (I will elaborate on this more in the next section.) And the jump into a human frame filled with heartwarming sentiment doesn't even need to entail live-action photography: in some films that are animation from beginning to end, the rendition of human toy owners in a less cartoony style (less stretchy, for example) than their toys can sentimentalize the human realm as less fantasy-based, more honest and down-to-earth, more anodyne, and more emotionally authentic than the cartoonish world of the toys in their own animate existence. Thus, at the end of *UglyDolls* (2019), the little girl who's been given the seemingly inanimate Moxie hugs her to her chest as Moxie, with a sentience unbeknownst to her new owner, looks knowingly and happily at us.

Yet, it is noteworthy that in *The LEGO Movie* (as well as some other films about animate toys, as we'll see), the seeming intrusion of Human Reality doesn't bring the fantasy of the toys as possessing life to an end: in these narratives, the toys continue to be alive even as the humans regard them as supposedly inanimate playthings. The move to the human frame doesn't end the fiction so much as blur it and "reality" in a new manner. Even after photographic reality has been introduced in *The LEGO Movie*, the animated story continues to unfold with its own level of fictional reality: we still see animate Emmet continuing his heroic efforts within his constructed LEGO world. And within an industrial logic that demands of *The LEGO Movie* that it be imagined as the first installment of a franchise and movie *series*, this first saga of Emmet can't end with him turning out to be nothing but an inanimate toy, his adventures nothing but a visualization of the stories the human Finn has imagined for him: in the last sequence of the film, we cut back, inevitably perhaps, from live-action, in which the dad tells Finn that if he wants to play creatively with the LEGO in the basement then his sister gets to play with them also, to animation of Emmet and his buddies confronted by an invasion of chirpy, animate DUPLO brought into their universe by the sister. *The LEGO Movie 2* can then proceed from that very ending, and it also concludes within the fictional world of animate toys (rather than in the human frame, that is): *after* a sentimental finale in the "real" world (the mom, played by Maya Rudolph, sees Finn and his sister able to play together with LEGO and DUPLO, and smiles contentedly), we are offered close to two minutes of animated depiction of the toys celebrating together in their now wonderfully mashed-up cartoon universe. In other words, humans might stand as the framing characters for toy play, but narratively *The LEGO Movie* (and its sequel) frame the humans themselves within a world of fantasy that seems to be able to go on and on.

Of course, even as a break to live-action, the end scenes between the humans don't give us Reality so much as another imagistic version of reality. For instance, I think it matters that the two adults of *The LEGO Movie* and *The LEGO Movie 2* are played by alums of *Saturday Night Live*, Will Ferrell and Maya Rudolph. The transition out of purely digital images to the scenes with these human actors is not fully a move to some unmediated reality outside manufactured screen spectacle, free of media influence. As Will Ferrell comes down the stairs in a slow reveal toward the end of *The LEGO Movie*, you can't ever forget that you're watching not the real father of a real family, but a well-known comic figure *play-acting* at being a stern patriarch (and if you see the film in a movie theater, you might hear squeals of delight from viewers when he first appears in the live-action scene). Any possible tug at the heartstrings as the father opens up to his son's creativity has necessarily to be held in check by our awareness of this as performance and as media-referential joke. (Likewise, the "reality" of the mother in *The LEGO Movie 2* is undone by such comic bits as Maya Rudolph stepping painfully onto some LEGO pieces and, as a comedian, overdoing the hurt she is feeling.)[5]

But if the intrusion of photographic reality doesn't really bring Authenticity to the *LEGO* movies, it's also the case that the converse—the film's luxuriating in digital fantasy—isn't just about pure escapism. In their very digitality, animated films can offer consequential comment on the nature of images in our lives. We should never make too much of this—we know always that whatever *The LEGO Movie* is "about," it's first of all about visual entertainment centered on little toy pieces to whom a lot of exciting things happen—but it's part of the mix, along with the irony, the comedy, the downright "big concept" movie idea of little figures in an epic saga. And one of the most resonant ideas as we watch movies with character toys such as LEGO minifigs is that maybe, somewhere inside them, lurks life indeed, and it's not all a mere game.

The Secret Life of Toys

When we play with toys, we impart possibility to them; we animate them; we can even pretend to give them something that resembles sentient being. And there's sometimes the uncanny sense that they have this life already within them, just lurking below their inanimate physicality as promise and potentiality. A long-running tradition of movies and TV shows about toys actualizes this suspicion and chronicles what happens when toys actually have lives or come to take on life.

Like some other films and television shows that chronicle the adventures of toys seemingly come to life (or endowed with life from the get-go), *The LEGO Movie* actually derives much of its impact from the blend of two narrative worlds that the conceit requires: one in which the toys are indeed imagined as beings imbued with some sort of life (whether biological or mechanical, or some mixture thereof), and one in which they are simply toys—inanimate objects there for humans to do with as they wish (play with, cherish, discard, destroy, and so on). Within this tradition, though, *The LEGO Movie* makes its own particular and particularly astute contribution by bracketing off the framing human world for the longest time (even as it gives hints of it, as noted earlier), seeming thereby to immerse us fully in the self-containment of a narrative world unfolding as if inhabited by minifigs who have "real" lives of their own. The film sets up this fictional premise, though, to give impact to its big reveal: namely, that these are indeed humanly possessed toys with no full life of their own. The reveal comes as a big revelation indeed to the spectator, but also to the minifig protagonist himself, and in the uniqueness of this narrative conceit amongst other films and TV shows centered on toys, *The LEGO Movie* turns out to belong also to a resonant tradition, going beyond animation and toys alone, about what it means to discover your very identity is a construct, that you are a puppet of some sort. Fundamentally, the big reveal is also the revelation that the entire LEGO narrative has been crafted by Finn, the boy—enacted, designed, directed, constructed, *and* deconstructed by him. If many toy films are about the impact of toy animation on the humans (the happiness, for instance, that the toys can maneuver to bring to the humans), *The LEGO Movie* is more about the consequences of human-toy interaction for the minifigures who imagined theirs was the only world.

The break between a "real" world of humans interacting with toy objects and a self-contained fictional world in which toys live on their own isn't necessarily absolute, and there can be bleeds from one to the other. *The LEGO Movie*, for instance, is replete with moments where human activity pops into the fictional space: for instance, after Vitruvius is beheaded (something that can happen to LEGO minifigs in the real world as well!), he returns as a cobbled-together figure dangled on a string, held by Finn, the boy in the real world who is intervening in the land of the LEGO. But the full import of these hints of a human realm beyond the self-contained LEGO fiction is not evident until the last act.

Obviously, *The LEGO Movie* intends, despite its peppering into the narrative of such hints of a human existence outside the toys' enclosed fictional world, for that big reveal to be a momentous surprise to viewers. That can happen only if we are able in our minds to separate, for a time, the two worlds, or to bracket out one world, the human one that serves as narrative frame to the other. In other words, we've got to imagine a world where LEGO figures fully have life, in and of themselves. We've got to not imagine (or not fully imagine) that however animate the LEGO are within their narrative world, they are nothing but toys in another world, that of humans who play with them. We're able to do this in large part because we are in fact used to fully enclosed stories of fully animate toys. And by doing this, we are able to let *The LEGO Movie* upset the common convention.

This is why I referred several paragraphs previously to "some other" TV shows and movies that depict toys endowed with life. If *The LEGO Movie* is all about admitting two levels of narrative while for the longest time obscuring the existence of one, and then creating dramatic effect when each bleeds into the other, some other toy films, as we will see, actually sever the connection between human world and toy world to give us fictions of toy characters with full lives of their own, disconnected from any human presence.

In this section, then, I want, as a means of getting at the distinguishing qualities of *The LEGO Movie*, to offer broader thoughts on some ways toys come to life in mainstream moving-image culture. This will at times mean leaving *The LEGO Movie* behind for a momentary look at other films and TV shows that are doing something a bit different, but leaving in a manner that then allows us to return to *The LEGO Movie* and capture the particularity of its toy conceit. There are so many examples out there of narratives of enlivened toys that it is probably not possible to be encyclopedic: I confess, for instance, that I haven't had the fortitude to go fully through the many iterations of *GI Joe* and many other toy-based popular moving-image narratives—which exist, especially, as endless hours of multiple cartoon series on TV along with live-action and animated films. What matters, more than a dry list, is to isolate some revealing possibilities and permutations in the moving-image life of toys.

But before looking at some toy narratives that pretend to bracket out the human world fully in order to imagine toys with self-contained lives (who therefore literally are not playthings), it's worth mentioning in passing an unsurprising, converse possibility that is much more everyday and ordinary: films set in the human world that simply show humans interacting with inanimate toys. To be obvious, toys are normally in our modern world, so it is normal to find them in films of modern human life. Even here, though, things can get interesting if there's the slightest hint that the toys may possess glimmers, or more, of sentience, feeling, emotion, and other qualities of life. On the one hand, there are all those uncanny and unsettling narratives about toys come to life for nefarious purposes: for example, the Chucky or Annabelle films, or the tight episode of *The Twilight Zone* where the doll "Talking Tina" threatens death to the patriarch of the family and then acts on her evil promise. (Conversely, *Vzpoura hraček*, a 1946 Czech stop-motion animation that celebrates liberation from German rule, offers a unique *political* take on the motif of the toy menacingly come to life: in this short, a Nazi on night patrol in occupied territory comes into a toymaker's shop only to have all the toys animate and attack him, driving him off.)

On the other hand, there's the whimsy of the 1939 film *Bachelor Mother*, where, as befits the film's status as screwball comedy, the would-be lovers (a scion of a large department store and one of the store's low-level clerks) keep breaking off their romance, and the woman goes into hiding only for the two to be reunited at the film's finale when a mechanical toy duck the woman has brought home for the child she is fostering suddenly starts to move around the flat with loud quacking, alerting the man to his beloved's presence and seeming thereby to have some agency and intentionality in the fostering and finalizing of the love match.[1]

From early on in movie history, the paradoxes of animated toys, when they are indeed imagined to be animate, are well on display. Canonic in this respect is the 1907 Edwin S. Porter one-reeler *The "Teddy" Bears*, a film well appreciated in cinema scholarship for its contradictions around gender, power, the status of cultural outsiders, and so on.[2] Based on a bear doll craze that Teddy Roosevelt inspired, *The "Teddy" Bears* inserts modern-day consumerism around toys into the classic fairy tale of Goldilocks. Thus, before Goldilocks goes into the bears' bedroom for her nap, as per the original tale, there is a striking sequence wherein she looks through the keyhole of a locked door and sees teddy bears that, as she watches, come to life in close-up and do acrobatics (through photographic frame-by-frame animation). This animation of the bears makes Goldilocks want so desperately to possess them that she tries to violently pry open the locked door, but to no avail. It is this effort that tires her out and leads her to seek out a soft bed.

There is evidence that the film was shown in department stores as well as movie theaters as a means to inspire teddy sales. In this respect, the striking animated sequence that brings the toys to dynamic life under Goldilocks's gaze (and ours, as the film offers a close view of the bears framed by the keyhole) can serve as tie-in promotion: we become as fascinated by energized teddies as Goldilocks is, even as we know that possession of such stuffies in our world would come, obviously, without all the acrobatics.

The film's ending, so shocking to modern sensibilities, has Goldilocks flee the bear family and enlist a hunter (who looks like Teddy Roosevelt) in her cause. He kills the bear parents, enslaves Baby Bear, and grants Goldilocks the teddies she's fantasized about. This raw outcome makes explicit the peremptory act of possession—here associated with the hunter's resemblance to Teddy Roosevelt, a veritable imperial actor—that can be seen to underlie human ownership of toys.

In contrast to the straightforwardness of stories that simply show inanimate toys in *our* world or the uncanny narratives of toys come to life *in the presence of humans*, many movies and television shows fully immerse us in a fictional world of toys that have self-contained existence. Think, for instance, of TV series like *GI Joe* and its feature film counterparts, or *Thomas the Tank Engine*, or the *Transformers* movies. These are all based on purchasable toys, but the narrative conceit is that the titular characters are animate beings exclusively, not themselves playthings for humans.[3] Interestingly, *Thomas* and the *Transformers* films include human beings within their fictional world, *but it is a single fictional world that the animate "toys" also exist in.* In other words, we see Transformers interact with humans, and we see the sentient trains transport humans and be greeted by them, but the Transformers and train cars are never assumed to be toys (hence, the quotation marks in the previous sentence). A potential paradox, then, can arise: these beings live in a world that supposedly bears much of the same reality as our human one, except that the "toy" characters are derived from actual toys that are outside the fiction, and that therefore can't also be in that fiction. To give a practical example, in their feature films, the Transformers enter a live-action world that is supposed to be ours in the real here-and-now—and it's a world filled with seemingly all the goods that we associate with our world—but no one in that world collects or plays with Transformers toys: these toys alone can have no existence there. (In like fashion, no human on the Isle of Sodor in *Thomas the Tank Engine* collects toy-size versions of the trains they ride in and greet as fellow beings at train stations.) In such cases, when toys become characters, any reminder of their toyness has to be left behind, bracketed out.[4]

Interestingly, the earliest movies in the live-action Transformers franchise emphasize the suburban materialism of the human protagonist—a teenage white boy who fits the many stereotypes of an adolescence geared to guy-driven acquisition (he wants a cool car, he'd love to have the cool babe, and so on). The films are all about possession and its pursuit, but the one commodity that can figure *nowhere* in the fiction, and therefore cannot be an object of desire within it, is the original Transformer toy such as we might buy in *our* world. Likewise, the 2017 live-action movie *Bratz*, which chronicles the high school adventures of four teenagers (derived, obviously, from the Bratz line of empowered girl dolls), revolves around the acquisition and possession of consumer goods. Theirs is a world of bedrooms resplendent with girl products and closets filled with clothes, but with no dolls to be found anywhere. In the absence of the dolls themselves, the film sells visual spectacle per se (lots of clothes, lots of musical numbers, lots of bright colors that pop off the screen), but this perhaps seemed too removed from direct promotion of the Bratz line to make a difference (the film was a notorious bomb, and its targeted audience largely stayed away; after several floundering make-overs of the Bratz dolls themselves, the product line appears to have gone into hiatus).[5]

Yet it is worth noting that many TV shows and films (including the *Bratz* movie) that imagine toys as characters in a self-contained narrative world and that make no reference to their original toy status often include a sort of enumerative moment that shows off and lists all these characters based ultimately on toys: the military setting of *GI Joe* literally allows for a roll call, but we might also witness a comparable cataloguing when, for one narrative reason or another, every tie-in character needs be to accounted for (for instance, in *My Little Pony*, the Princess calls one-by-one to the ponies that she hopes will help her in planning a glorious celebration).

Such enumeration of characters can serve plot points (all these figures need indeed to be enlisted in a mission of some sort), but it also perhaps functions to remind the viewer of the toys that can be purchased in the real world outside the movie theater (sometimes directly outside the theater, at the concession stand). It is noteworthy that opening credits for some toy-based films or TV shows whose narratives proper never recognizes them as toys are sometimes more likely to acknowledge their extra-filmic toy existence, as if more explicit salesmanship for the toys is permitted before the story gets underway (for example, the LEGO DVD movie *Bionicle: The Mask of Light* begins, before any other credits, with LEGO bricks swirling together to form the company's logo, a reminder of the building blocks that never come to be acknowledged in the movie proper). And some TV shows and films use opening credits to show off all the actual, real-world toys from the franchise so as to establish links between viewable characters on-screen and the purchasable off-screen toys they are derived from (for example, *Thomas the Tank Engine*, in which the opening song tells of the qualities of each train character one by one).[6]

As we've seen, *The LEGO Movie* frequently offers enumerative montages, but these are just too rapid to really stand as specific advertisements for physical LEGO items. Similarly, *The LEGO Batman Movie* parodies enumeration in a scene where Joker lists (and we see corresponding images of) the members of his evil cohort, each moniker flashing by and becoming more improbable to both Batman and us viewers (for example, could there really be a LEGO character or a DC villain named Condiment Man [aka Condiment King]?), inviting incredulity until Joker responds to the doubts by saying, "Google it." (For what it's worth, I did: Yes, Virginia, there is a Condiment Man, and Google offers numerous sites to clarify his backstory in DC comics and TV shows).[7] No doubt, fact-checking the names of the villains resolves suspicion but also connects us to the original minifigs back in a real world of possible acquisition.

Of course we buy toys, but through movie tickets or DVD acquisition or streaming, we also buy toy stories that flit before our eyes and that we don't necessarily possess physically. No doubt, the virtuality of the narratives that flash across screens in this manner can sometimes leave us with a frustrating sense of incompleteness or of incomplete possession (there are movies that seem to be racing away from us and turning into mere memories even as they unspool), and we can in some cases try to extend the experience through possession *of things* that will substitute for or remind us of the movie experience itself. For instance, in the days of the studio system, we could write away for glossies of the stars from the films. Or through the decades up to the present times we might have bought a toy associated with a movie, even when it only partially let us play at experiences the movie's toy-derived character was engaged in.

But in order to work its spell, toy ownership needs to be imagined as benign and free of such qualities as greed, the imperiousness of seizure, even the blunt act of economic possession. If the early *"Teddy" Bears* film makes explicit the violence in bringing a toy into a human life (Goldilocks gets her desired teddies only because the Bear parents are shot dead and Baby Bear enslaved), later representations predictably obfuscate the violence of possession, both physical and economic, and substitute the image of a loving relationship between humans and their toys. To be sure, forms of violence lurk at the edges of many toy tales, such as the violence of abandonment: most famous, no doubt, is the popular folksong "Puff the Magic Dragon," about a favored plaything that begins to be ignored when its owner grows up to prefer newer objects of amusement. Within works of animation, we find the motif of abandonment in several of the Raggedy Ann films: the Raggedy Ann short *The Eternal Square* from 1947 goes so far as to include under its single-shot opening credits a moment where we see an Ann doll thrown from off-screen and landing in the trash. Yet such films generally set up abandonment in order to then triumph over it through new, inspiring acts of proper ownership: for example, the tossed-away Raggedy Ann of *The Eternal Square* is rescued by a stereotypically cheerful Irish cop on the beat who gives her to a loving, blind waif.

Often, films about benign human possession of toys show them happily planted in the child's room from the start, or brought into that space not through imperial acquisition but the gentle process of gifting. Money relations are obscured for a more reassuring narrative of toys' "natural" introduction into children's lives (even as the narrative's ultimate goal may of course be to encourage that viewer to acquire through purchasing), although someone in the story world presumably had to at some point pay for these toys, something that *Toy Story 2* somewhat admits when it leaves Andy's bedroom for the toy store as initial point of purchase of toys, and that *The LEGO Movie* alludes to when in its live-action coda Finn mentions the toy store that the LEGO came from.[8]

One recurrent motif that brackets out acquisition as economic transaction is the toy that enters one's life through gifting at a birthday party: for instance, *Toy Story*, which seems directly inspired by the 1977 *Raggedy Ann and Andy* in its motifs of toys who always seem to have been ready and waiting in a child's room *and* the arrival of a new and somewhat petulant birthday toy who threatens to mess up existing child-toy relations but turns out to be a good addition after all. And *The Indian in the Cupboard*, from a revered children's story, is all about what happens when three birthday gifts—a statuette of a Native American, an old cupboard, and a key—come together so that the title character can come to life for the young boy who now has possession of him.

In this context, one of the few films to acknowledge that toys in a capitalist system might be expected to be paid for, the 1941 short *Raggedy Ann and Andy*, is revealing in the ways it raises monetary concerns only to dispense with them in favor of gifting as the most beneficial means (for child and toy alike) for ownership to occur. A little cherub comes up to the window of a toy store in what appears to be a quaint old-style village (a clue already that venal capitalist considerations will ultimately be left to the side) and admires the two sewn-together Raggedy dolls (Andy and Ann) in the window, on sale for a dollar. She's clearly been pining for Ann for a long time and enters the shop to offer the shopkeeper 50 cents (all she has in the world, we learn) for just the girl doll. Declaring that he can't separate the two dolls and therefore must have the whole dollar, the shopkeeper tells the origin story of how the two dolls were fabricated and went on an adventure that made them realize they were emotionally inseparable. This recounted tale becomes a story-within-the-framing story and we see, visualized, the narrative of the dolls' production and then their entrance into the world (they discover that they've left the factory without having been named and go off on a quest to find their monikers; it is on this journey that the boy doll gets separated from the girl doll and both realize they must always stay together). Revealingly, the factory sequence is itself a veritable mythologizing of commodity production: there is little glimpse of mass production here as the two raggedy dolls seem to be the only items to come off the assembly line, and the instruments that fabricate them are themselves anthropomorphized animated characters who thereby shake off some of the cold anonymity of the factory system.

Once this framed narrative ends, we return to the shop, where we see that the little girl has understood, if somewhat begrudgingly, why she can't have just one doll and at half the full price. But as she trudges away in acceptance of the ways of the world, the shopkeeper suddenly feels beneficent and offers her both dolls as a gift. Monetary concerns hover over the tale but then get wished away.

Tellingly, for *The LEGO Movie*, there is no detailed depiction of how the stereotypically suburban father got so much LEGO stuff—and it's indeed A LOT. The viewer probably just assumes that this sort of middle-class white dad easily has the means. As noted, Finn mentions visiting the store where the LEGO were acquired, but there's little more than that quick reference. By bracketing out any deeper engagement with economics, the film displaces the violence of possession into the different threat that these already possessed toys might be fixed into place (Kragled) and robbed of all ability (in their world) to animate and (in the human world) to be combined in ever more creative constructions.

Here, we may compare *The LEGO Movie* to its most obvious forebear, *Toy Story* (with sequels in 1999, 2010, and 2019). *Toy Story* is in many ways a compendium of the motifs I've been enumerating in the last pages. There's the theme of gifting (Buzz Lightyear enters the story as a birthday present) but also, conversely, potential abandonment of a toy (for instance, when Woody's arm gets damaged severely in *Toy Story 2*, he has a horrific nightmare of being thrown by Andy into the trash; cowgirl Jessie, we learn, was indeed abandoned when her first owner outgrew her). If the films in the series center on the idea that toys come to life when humans are out of the room, there's also the rule-breaking moment (identified as such by Woody and authorized by him) when toys animate in front of a human (the sadistic kid Sid in the first film) to threaten him and scare him away. There's the heartwarming sentiment that for every toy there's a special owner (even as the third film deals wistfully with kids growing up and growing out of their childhood devotions, and the fourth misleads the spectator for a while as to who is the destined owner of the forlorn Gabby Gabby doll). And there's the veritable existential trauma that ensues when a sentient character who thought they had full control of their being finds they are nothing but a plaything for humans: this is the discovery that Buzz makes in the initial film when he happens on a television advertisement about his product line (conversely, Woody's discovery, in the second film, that he is based on a very influential kid's TV show enthralls him rather than shocking him to his existential core).[9]

Yet the very sentimentality of the *Toy Story* series is ultimately quite different from what we are given in *The LEGO Movie*. It's not merely that much of the knowing irony I've outlined in *The LEGO Movie* is less apparent in the *Toy Story* franchise, despite its own moment-to-moment awareness of the commodified nature of toys. Some of the difference has to do, I would suggest, with the very idea of the LEGO minifig and the way that is used in the movie. For all the joy we can take in playing with LEGO, it might well be that they don't invite love and emotional devotion and sentiment in the same way many other anthropomorphized toys do.

As physical toys, LEGO bricks and accessories have a unique status. On the one hand, as elements to be assembled together in construction, LEGO offer the possibility of non-character creations built up from often pure geometric shapes, with their basic shape as their only identity (the brick is a brick)—and in that, they resemble the characterless pieces of, say, Erector sets or Lincoln logs. Here, there is probably little possibility for direct emotional involvement by the owner with the toy (that is, we could perhaps invest them with personality, but the pieces are inert and characterless). Yet with LEGO the minifigs do bring the potential for introducing character (and then narrative and emotion) into the constructed space. Even so, their scale (the minifigs are only about an inch tall) and the very fact of their constructedness (their owner knowingly has put them together), combined perhaps with their hardness (as plastic toys, they are not flexibly cuddly), probably makes them less a potential target for the sort of sentimental love children direct toward the larger, fully formed character-like dolls and squishy stuffies they are wont to connect with deeply (and, for example, to curl up in bed with or hug to their chest, as in the last scene of *UglyDoll*).[10] True, when we finally see the human realm toward the end of *The LEGO Movie*, Finn appears to have a special regard for Emmet (the boy stares at the minifig intently as if trying to find a life within), and maybe even some sort of ineffable bond with him, but Emmet finally is little more than a somewhat random element in Finn's constructed universe, relegated to the basement, easily lost, and inviting little affect from the humans, Finn and his father alike, who manipulate him, for good or bad.

The LEGO Movie is, in its depiction of how humans relate to toys, likely more hard-edged (pun intended) in emotional tone than many other films about animate toys. This is due, I think, to the very nature of the LEGO minifig as the sort of character the film builds its narrative upon. True, there is sentimentality on exhibit in the film, but it tends to be expressed less between the human world *and* the LEGO fictional one than between inhabitants in each of these realms *among themselves*. That is, this is not about humans hugging lovable dolls as play-friends they cannot live without. This is not about the assertion that for every child, there is one special doll or toy (and vice versa—that for every toy, there is one child out there waiting for them). Within the human realm of *The LEGO Movie*, sentiment is expressed between members of a family (dad and son in the first film, brother and sister in the second, with mom looking on in emotional contentment). Within the LEGO realm, figures can care about each other. But between the worlds, there is little emotional connection, and, of course, for much of the first film, the minifigs don't even know of the human realm. Ironically, though, for all the emotional affect on display in the *Toy Story* films, it may well be that *The LEGO Movie*, by resorting to live-action photography for its scenes of humans, actually is more effective at rendering people than the films of the *Toy Story* franchise—which notoriously offer up computer-generated versions of humans that are, it must be said, downright clumsy in visual style. Even as they engage in narratives rich in sentiment, the *Toy Story* humans look and move like awkward caricatures, yet still they tug at our heartstrings.[11]

By holding off the big reveal that the LEGO are human-owned toys and depicting them until then as fully animate beings in their own world (despite occasional hints of the human frame world), *The LEGO Movie* revises in clever and resonant fashion the tradition of toys that come to life in a human world. As we've seen, most toy stories that are also the stories of the humans who interact with them start with a purportedly real world in which humans bear a relation to toys they can manipulate: in some such cases, the toys come to life in their presence (for example, those creepy dolls that start talking to humans); in others, the toys try to wait for the humans to be away before they, the toys, start to animate (for instance, in

Toy Story or the 1977 *Raggedy Ann and Andy* feature film).[12] Somewhat apart from these options, but still about the transition from "real life" to "fantasy world of live toys" is the dismal case of *The Playmobil Movie* (2019), where a brother and sister play with Playmobil toys in a live-action prologue only to be sucked into an animated world of Playmobil locales populated by sentient figurines. There is little narrative logic or motivation to the transformation other than that the film crassly needs to get the kids—and us spectators—to this commodity world of toys on display. At the other extreme are films that bracket out any framing human world where the toys are just toys, to offer instead the fiction of a self-contained world of characters who are themselves supposed to be fully sentient beings (such as GI Joe).

While *The LEGO Movie* does have those fascinating early hints where bits of the framing human world break into the fictional space of LEGO in which the toys are supposedly animate, sentient beings, for the longest time the minifigs within the fictional world of *The LEGO Movie* don't know that they ultimately, fundamentally, are nothing but toys. This is in contrast to, say, the Batman of *The LEGO Batman Movie*, who is never imagined to be a toy (even though he seems to be the same Batman as in *The LEGO Movie*), but also to the toy and doll characters in *Toy Story* and *Raggedy Ann and Andy*, who know they are lifeless toys in the eyes of their human owners and have to act as such when aware humans are around. Not following either of these options, *The LEGO Movie* offers something closer, perhaps, to the existential dilemmas that fictional characters who think they are fully existing beings in and of themselves confront when they discover that they have been fabricated (for instance, the cyborg Rachel of *Blade Runner*, who had long believed she was fully human, or the clones of Kazuo Ishiguro's novel *Never Let Me Go* [2005], or, in another way, Truman in *The Truman Show*, who is not literally a construction but discovers that his humanity has been manipulated since birth for the purposes of spectacle for the people of the world).[13]

Emmet may have a vague awareness of a "man upstairs" who has some sort of influence over the denizens of the LEGO world, but his assumption is that this figure of power exists in the same narrative world that he's in—and not somehow outside of it (in other words, the Man Upstairs might just be an even more powerful LEGO figure). Of course, for long stretches, the film encourages this assumption by showing the ruling figure of Emmet's world (and of the adjacent ones he wanders into) to be a LEGO minifig himself, President Business (eventually renamed Lord Business, given how many worlds he tries to control). For Emmet, the only world he knows is the LEGO one, built up as it is out of pieces that are normal and natural to him (hence, he is not shocked that he has clasps for hands—that's reality in the fiction he's in) and controlled by Lord Business. Even when he's thrown from one LEGO land to another, Emmet never doubts his own existence as a sentient being in those lands. When the dimensions of his LEGO universe start to expand (for instance, when Wyldstyle transports him into a LEGO Old West), the leap is into an adjacent world, not one on a different plane of existence.

For LEGO minifigs in the film, there is nothing beyond the LEGO universe they believe they fully exist within. And this comes with an intriguing side implication, one given stunning visual representation in the film: there can be no Nature here but one built up of LEGO pieces. The sky, the seas, the other elements, are all LEGO.

This is again quite different from the tradition that *Toy Story* derives from. As in many other similar narratives, the human world in *Toy Story* is most centrally localized as a kid's *bedroom*—one filled with toys that, when humans are out of the way, can come to life, and in which they can feel literally at home. Notably, though, these toys are often sent on quests that force them to move into alien spaces, beyond the bedroom, that are often new and, thereby, often foreboding to them, and that they have to navigate and brave dangers and adventures in, only to return home, so they hope, at the film's end. Indeed, the narrative motif of a window that serves as a threshold out of the humans' house and that the toys must fearfully venture out of (or accidentally fall from) is common to these films. *Small Soldiers* offers an ironic variant in which the sentient toy-creatures, the Gorgons, dream of returning to their home, which they believe lies somewhere far beyond the human bedroom whose window they look longingly out of, but what they are questing for are simply idyllic images of a verdant paradise that were shown on a television in the humans' home and that the Gorgons mistakenly imagined to be where they came from: in other words, their very nostalgia for a succoring natural refuge has been mass produced for them.

The LEGO Movie does hint at spaces beyond the built LEGO universe its characters move in (but don't know has been built for them), yet it remains little more than a hint (the furthest we get from the basement in the first film of the franchise is a glimpse of stairs coming down from the rest of the humans' house). *The LEGO Movie 2* goes a bit farther by taking us into other parts of the humans' house and even the backyard, yet it may be noteworthy that when LEGO are brought out of the basement by Finn and his sister, they remain inanimate toys in an essentially safe space—the back-yard as a place of playful celebration. But because *The LEGO Movie* works initially from the conceit that its LEGO are full beings in their own right, and because the film therefore brackets out any acknowledgment of a human frame (such as a bedroom), at the outset it doesn't show domestic human space—and to make the big reveal work, it can't. (We might contrast this to the opening of *Toy Story*, which offers careful exploration of Andy's room and then an inventory of the sentient toys within it, confirming from the start the importance of the human frame.)

The basement frames the LEGO universe, and it is within that human space that their fictional narratives transpire, but that's something we learn only at the film's end.[14] Within the fictional space, there can be no space beyond (whether a bedroom or, way beyond that, through a window), and every-thing is made up of LEGO—not merely the characters but also their environments, natural and otherwise. The minifigs live within a complete LEGO-ization of everything. One telling exception to the total containment of minifigs within the LEGO fiction comes once the human frame has been acknowledged: Emmet, by animating himself on a table in the basement real world (and then falling off it), breaks through to human reality to enlist human Finn's help in his cause within the LEGO universe. Notably, though, he can fall off the table, but still remains confined to the basement. He is never thrown into the greater world beyond, as happens in the quest narrative of *Toy Story* and its forebears.

In a way, this spread of a LEGO vision to all corners of reality—so that even "nature" comes to be made up of LEGO pieces—is an astute mirroring of the very philosophy of LEGO play itself. I'll talk more about the history of the LEGO company in the next section, but for the moment it's worth noting how, starting in the 1950s, the LEGO bricks, which at that time were only one product line for the company, came to be treated as the *core* product and then came to supplant other offerings. Strikingly, books on the LEGO phenomenon often invest in a language of totalization and expansion—LEGO can be everywhere, everything can be pulled into a LEGO way of life (and that's generally all for the better). For instance, Sara Herman in her "unofficial" (yet fully respectful) history, *A Million Little Bricks*, tells us early on that the "LEGO world is bigger than its design and manufacturing processes," while David Robertson in his encomium to LEGO as a model business goes so far as to imagine LEGO as a force so powerful it converts human reality to its look: "Billund [where TLG has its corporate headquarters] itself is a toy town, you might say . . . The neat rows of yellow-brick houses, topped with red-tile roofs, have the symmetry and stolidity of a little LEGO streetscape. . . . Watching staffers [in LEGO headquarters] bustle along the neon-red and yellow hallways, it's easy to imagine them as LEGO minifigures, with those sunny skin tones and preternaturally happy faces. If there is such a thing as a factory of fun, it is here, in Billund."[15] The human world itself starts to seem a LEGO creation that extends itself everywhere.

The breakthrough for TLG in the 1950s was not just to home in on the brick, but to understand that that rectangular piece harbored a potential for endless expansion. In what histories of the company treat as a veritable revolution in toy philosophy, in 1954 corporate head Godtfred Kirk Christiansen termed the brick the key component in a "System of

Play": no longer a neutral array of discrete pieces played with, each in its own manner, but an endlessly built and built-up universe grown and growing ever larger and ever more expansive. One might start with a box set that included buildings, props (trees, street lamps, etc.), and vehicles, with the possibility of always obtaining more pieces to extend the set into ever greater and grander complexity. Some sets even came with studded mats so that worlds could be built up out of a veritable ground or grounding. As Maaike Lauwaert summarized the System of Play in one of the key studies of LEGO, "[P]layers could design and construct more and would want more elements of the LEGO play system. Instead of the child having a multitude of individual toys, the System of Play allowed children to combine all the LEGO toys that belonged to the System."[16]

What if there were nothing to the universe but LEGO and LEGO-like characters? This is the universe (including adjacent LEGO worlds) that *The LEGO Movie* constructs and that those characters inhabit. Given that it's their universe pure and simple, they would themselves never "think" to ask such a question about the boundaries of existence.

But of course the human world—our world as LEGO brick buyers, our world as LEGO moving-image consumers—lies just beyond. And the cleverness of *The LEGO Movie* is to keep that world beyond at bay for as long as possible to make its ultimate reveal provide an upheaval to the tradition of films about toys come to life.

Production History, Part 1:

Project Development as LEGO Goes to the Movies

One strand of the production history of *The LEGO Movie* has to do with The LEGO Group coming on board with the very idea of a feature-length work about physical toys. The film wasn't an official production of TLG, but a project licensed from them by Warner Bros. and developed by the studio's Animation Group, for which it became their first released feature. Screenwriters Dan and Kevin Hageman, who had previously scripted *Hotel Transylvania* (and who would go on to further LEGO involvement as writers and producers of episodes of the Ninjago TV show), were hired to write the treatment. They came up with the breakthrough premise of animation giving way in the film's last part to live-action. (In their version, Emmet was an architect, and one item that fell into his LEGO world from the human one was a sock).

At one point, Michel Gondry—who in 2002 had made an acclaimed LEGO music video for White Stripes' "Fell in Love with a Girl"—was courted to direct the feature film, but that fell through. Producer Dan Lin talked with Phil Lord and Chris Miller, who at first didn't think they were right for a

LEGO movie (and worried somewhat about it being too much of a commercial for LEGO), but nonetheless gave him loads of ideas that clearly resonated.

With the overall concept from the Hageman treatment of a LEGO hero ultimately revealed to be a figure within the human world (but also with Lord and Miller's insights on how to expand that premise), Lin made a trip to LEGO corporate headquarters in Billund, Denmark, to sell the company on the idea of a movie. (Once the project was approved, he made several more trips, with Jill Wilfert, LEGO vice president of global licensing and entertainment, from the United States to work through production decisions with the Billund toy division.)[1] As Lin recounts of his first visit to pitch the film and TLG's subsequent involvement once they approved the idea, "Unlike many toy companies, LEGO didn't have to make a movie. It was very risky for them to do so because we were playing with their main brand, not one of their product lines. So the idea had to be the right one and it had to be executed at the highest level for this to work. Their main goal for the film was to build the LEGO brand and to branch out into storytelling. LEGO had script approval and was an integral part of the creative process. They were involved from start to finish, including rough cuts."[2] To demonstrate to the LEGO administrators at Billund how animation could work for LEGO minifigs (and also, eventually, to recruit directors Phil Lord and Chris Miller by showing what high-production animation of LEGO could achieve), Warner Bros. had Blur, an animation firm, do a two-minute test in which a generic minifig (like Emmet in overall look) searches through an Arctic wasteland for an explorer, Murphy, who's disappeared. He's found frozen but alive, in a block of ice. Just as his would-be rescuer is about to free him, a giant hand descends, and there is a cut to a live-action human world in which Murphy is revealed to be just a LEGO minifig inside an ice cube dropped into a glass of soda. Obviously, the plot is not that of the eventual LEGO feature film—and the demo doesn't include the latter's conceit that nature itself should be rendered in LEGO form. Yet the short film does capture the tension (one that is bracketed out for a while to make its reveal reverberate as a punch line to the entire narrative) between the animated LEGO world and the photographed human world that is so important to the feature film. Most importantly, it also shows how minifigs can be endowed with emotion (Murphy's eyes, for instance, "say" so much when he is found entrapped in the ice; his would-be savior's emotions run the gamut from wryness to determination to panic). When some of the possibilities Lin was pitching seemed to fall flat with LEGO executives, he pulled out Lord and Miller's ideas for expanding the overall premise, and these turned out to resonate.

Lin continued, as he put it, to "woo" director-writers Phil Lord and Chris Miller to take on *The LEGO Movie*. Lin was aware of their animated cult TV series *Clone High* and had also been impressed by how, in their feature debut, the animated film *Cloudy with a Chance of Meatballs*, Miller and Lord had, in his words, "showed they could create an original take on a film based on Intellectual Property that needed characters and story to be fleshed out in depth."[3]

In 2010, Miller and Lord agreed to take over scripting and directing. At multiple sites on the web, one can find two early LEGO scripts of theirs, each fairly similar to the other, with the overall framework for the final version already in place (ordinary Emmet as hero who saves the day), but with some

significant differences from what ultimately showed up on-
screen. For instance, Lucy is dating the LEGO pirate, not
Batman; the villain is not a fat capitalist, but a more traditional adversary named Black Falcon; and in the real world
the LEGO belong not to Finn's dad, but to his uncle, who the
young boy is visiting for the evening. Most strikingly, this early
iteration includes lively interaction between humans and the
LEGO minifigs, and comes up with a mother for Emmet—
Dolly, who turns out in fact to be the Chosen One (until she is
beaten down at the task and Emmet has to assume the role for
her). Unlike in the final version, this difference gives Emmet
a backstory (which includes him having "dated" Lucy in eighth
grade) and thereby alters his essential anonymity, which is so
important to the released film. It's almost as if the absence of
a father for Finn in the early script versions meant that familial sentiment had to be displaced into the deep relationship of
Emmet and Dolly.[4]

From the start, and through all versions of the script, Lord
and Miller were clear that they didn't want to come up with a
feature that would be little more than an extended commercial
for LEGO. As Miller put it in an interview around the film's
release, "Well, we were very clear up front that the only way
this movie was gonna succeed was if it didn't come from the
top down. It didn't feel like it was a corporate commercial. It
didn't feel like LEGO was saying, 'We wanna sell these toys,
tell a story around them.' It had to feel like it was coming from
outside the company. It was filmmaker and story driven and
that it was using LEGO as a medium. Now obviously, you
know, they're gonna wanna sell toys based on the movie. And
we said, obviously if we're making something that doesn't have
cool vehicles in it and interesting characters, then we're not

doing our job anyway. We're not gonna make a LEGO movie that isn't about cool LEGO stuff. And we went to Denmark to visit and see the type of things that they make there and it definitely inspired us from what LEGO's core values are about and the type of things. But we were thankfully not in a situation where they were dictating anything to us as far as what we were doing."[5]

Of course, The LEGO Group stood to benefit from all the tie-ins (such as *LEGO Movie*–themed construction sets), including some that would assume the form of moving-image media in their own right. For instance, as we'll see later, TLG commissioned its own short, a semi-sequel to the feature film, to show in its amusement parks and indoor Discovery centers.

TLG has in fact had a long-running history with moving images. But to tell that story, it is no doubt useful to outline the broader corporate history of LEGO. The story is both the specific one of how moving images entered into the world of LEGO, in the form of, early on, animated commercials and then low-budget TV series (for example, the well-known Ninjago and Chima series, redolent of Saturday-morning superhero TV for kids), and the longer saga of how the company came up with the very idea of the LEGO physical toy and then branched beyond it into new realms such as the moving image.

Yet the film and television history of LEGO perhaps needs to be separated somewhat from the company's digital turn, even though there is some chronological overlap (and even though, obviously, virtually all of the moving-image representations of LEGO would, by the twenty-first century, be on digital platforms). The digital turn entailed, for instance, TLG's development in the 1980s of programmable robotic playthings

(LEGO Mindstorms), which they promoted on the basis of their educational value, regarding software development and users' invention and refinement of programming languages. But, as we saw in earlier pages in this study, TLG pretty much imagined this sort of digital activity as being in a separate silo centered more on learning and learned construction, and differing strongly in intent from the mere watching of stories in movies and on television. Even the video games that spun off from the shows and films and that entailed active play by gamers were treated as somewhat apart from the passive watching that is endemic to TV and film consumption. Phil Lord and Chris Miller were consulted deeply on the video game for *The LEGO Movie* (made, as noted, by a gaming firm owned by Warner Bros.), but the efforts of Warner Animation to craft the unit's first animated feature appear themselves to have been treated as a separate process with its own integrity and particularity: the emphasis was on the making, in and of itself, of a narrative feature film that would stand on its own (even as it predictably would be tied to other LEGO products and indeed to the world of the brand overall). As Phil Lord put it to me, "From a physical production standpoint we were entirely separate [from the gaming unit] and took a different creative approach from the games. Theatrical animation and real time game rendering have different objectives and creative technical challenges."[6]

We need to keep that creative separateness of the film—what we might term its inevitable divergence as a movie from the convergence that represents LEGO as a brand and as a veritable world across all its iterations and embodiments—as we tell the broader story of LEGO and how moving-image culture came into its orbit. The chronicle starts with Ole Kirk Christiansen (1891–1958), a farmhand who apprenticed himself out as a carpenter and eventually opened his own woodworking business in Billund, Denmark, making furniture and even habitats for the population of this small, rural town. The Great Depression hit hard, and Christiansen added a product line of wooden toys (some with movable parts) to catch those customers whose children needed a bit of pleasure in dour times. Although some relatives looked down on the idea of toy manufacture, preferring more utilitarian applications of woodworking, and although Ole did indeed continue the carpentry side of the business, toys became central enough to the operation that in 1934 he named the entire operation LEGO, the Danish term for "play well" (but also, it turns out, Latin for "I put together" or "I assemble"). Whether in wood or, increasingly, in plastic, the first wave of toys from the company were primarily what we might term "play toys"—that is, fully finished items (or ones that required a minimal amount of assembly in order to attain their predetermined finality)—as opposed to "construction toys," centered more on the building process and allowing for a large degree of innovation in how they were to be put together.

Eventually, the wooden toy line (as well as any non-toy wooden products focused on utility rather than play) split off from the LEGO operation and was given its own name before being canceled completely in 1960. Beginning in the 1940s, one of Ole's sons, Godtfred Kirk Christiansen (known as GKC), had assumed greater responsibility for the family business and homed in on toys. A major breakthrough came in 1947 from the company's interest in developing more of its line in plastic. Plastic had been available for decades as a versatile material for light manufacture. Made from a molten substance, it allowed color to be mixed into it (rather than applied as fadeable or chippable paint to the surface); it allowed all sorts of new shapes to be developed; its light weight saved on shipping costs; it had great durability (many early LEGO bricks are still around and still linkable to later iterations); and molding it was a speedy mass-production operation once the matrices were fabricated. Above all, as plastic moved into the postwar age, it seemed fully *modern* and expressive of a time of dynamic expansion and exploration in a way that wood, for example, didn't. Plastic was sleek; its colors in toys seemed both radiant and artificial in a way that referenced high modernism (painter Piet Mondrian has been cited as the source for the original colors in LEGO bricks); and, when molded into pared-down geometric shapes like the brick, it evoked the pure rationality of the modernist aesthetic and social project, such as the nonornamental and sleekly mathematical angularity of the built architectural environments of International Modernism. (From stark skyscrapers like the Seagram Building to *2001: A Space Odyssey*'s alien monolith, the pure and unadorned rectangle stands as the perfect incarnation of modernist higher reason.)

At great expense to the company, Ole and Godtfred ordered an advanced plastic-injection molding machine from the United Kingdom that could speed up regularized production of plastic elements. No doubt, their original intent was to obtain a technology to make fully constructed *play toys* that required no assemblage at the consumer's end, but the promotional material that had come with the machine included mention of stackable and interlockable bricks that a British child psychologist, Hilary Fisher Page, had invented for his own toy company, Kiddicraft, and that he had made with the molding machine. This possibility called to the Danes.

Page had termed the basic element the "Interlocking Building Cube," and each cube had a series of studs on top that allowed a successive cube to be fitted onto it (but the inner bottom side in Page's version was simply empty, so there was no permanence to the connection of one brick to another). The patents for Page's invention did not extend to Denmark, so Ole and Godtfred essentially took over the basic concept (a fact Godtfred conceded many years later in a legal battle over patents, eventually settled out of court) and refined it, sharpening the edges and working on the clutch of one brick to another. By 1949, TLG was using its molding machine almost exclusively for the production of linkable cubes, which they named Automatic Binding Bricks. In 1957—a year celebrated in histories of the company—Godtfred brought to the Danish patent office a most consequential refinement of the brick: complementing the studs on top, the bricks now sported an additional series of tubes *in their under-chassis*, and the combined stud-and-tube arrangement, as it came to be called, allowed the bricks to be *snapped together* in tight fashion. Godtfred had already in 1954 lauded the notion of a LEGO System of Play (described earlier), which was in very large part about imagining the building up of ever-expansive worlds, and the stud-and-tube process gave the idea its full potential.

From the 1960s into the 1980s, LEGO continued to develop expandable play sets, although the company also included an increasing number of themed sets with larger, noninterchangeable elements, custom-designed around a specific theme, that would encourage users to follow fixed paths in the fabrication of worlds and vehicles (the latter got a boost in 1961 when the company developed wheels that could be connected via axles to bricks, thus enabling a move away from the fully prefabricated vehicles that had accompanied box sets up until then). More and more, for instance, sets came to include pieces (such as windshields or vehicle chassis) that were pre-formed in order to be constructible according to only one pathway (i.e., if you didn't build according to a part's predestined fit into the kit, you couldn't really use the element to build the desired model), and the company even began in 1964 to include building instructions (visual images only, without words, in order to work across cultures) for many of its kits, as if again to indicate the proper way to build a model to a planned goal.

But at the same time that it was perhaps mandating "proper" construction, TLG was showing itself to be open to broader development beyond the LEGO system itself. A significant product innovation, for instance, was DUPLO, introduced in 1969: these were bricks and accessories double-sized in every dimension to the original LEGO bricks (hence, the doubling reference in the name) so that younger children could play with them. A somewhat parallel venture by TLG was to develop simplified product lines for girls, as it was assumed that boys were more interested in large-scale construction. Of course, DUPLO and girl appeal as new directions for TLG come together pointedly at the end of *The LEGO Movie*, where we discover that Finn's younger sister plays with DUPLO (and brings them into Finn's LEGO world), and throughout much of *The LEGO Movie 2*, which initially is all about seeming conflict between LEGO and DUPLO. Obviously, the resolution of the second movie, in keeping with the broader corporate concerns of TLG, is to assert that the different product lines can not only exist together but can also work together *and merge together* (in fact, from the start, actual DUPLO were designed to be lockable to LEGO so that compatibility was never a problem).

In 1988, Godtfred's son Kjeld Kirk Kristiansen (the reason for the change in spelling of his surname is unclear) took over the business, keeping it a family concern. The 1990s saw TLG responding to a new world of child's play—increasingly, screen-based and digitalized—by expanding the range of physical sets but also by *embracing the world of screens themselves* as places for playful investment of spectators in the LEGO world. There would still be physical LEGO, but there would also be an exerted and extended move into other areas such as moving-image and often digitalized platforms. These new ventures provide direct context for *The LEGO Movie*.

TLG had been involved in moving-image production from at least the 1950s, when it used TV to advertise physical LEGO.[7] Some of the commercials animated LEGO vehicles and figures through photographic stop-motion (in the UK, one advertisement with famed comedian Tommy Cooper, in which he voices a competition between two LEGO creatures that endlessly morph to try to triumph over the other, is still revered). But in some national contexts, there were restrictions on images of seemingly self-animating toys, as it was felt this might lead consumers to imagine that the toys actually moved on their own. One solution was to emphasize the toy owners, shown in live-action and waving this or that item around in their hands. In the case of LEGO in the US market, this led to some celebrity in the 1980s for one such imputed owner, Zack the LEGO Maniac (later "Jack"), a young, cool dude in shades who danced around his bedroom and the school lunchroom with LEGO creations in hand. In 1987, LEGO tried a different tack for advertising its physical toy: it commissioned a collection of short (five minutes or so) episodes for a TV series called *Edward and Friends* that contained no direct advertising, but simply intended to put LEGO creatures in amusing situations. The plan was to pitch the show to the BBC, but it first ran afoul of aforementioned restrictions against stop-motion animation of toys (instead, the episodes were shot with claymation figures designed to look like LEGO, rather than plastic pieces themselves) and then was rejected anyway as too commercial. It had a limited life as a series sold to the Canadian market, but is noteworthy as the first venture by TLG to develop narrative in moving-image form as more than just explicit commercials. It is the antecedent to later successful LEGO series like *Chima* and *Ninjago* and *Bionicles* (as well as the less-enduring *Clutch Powers*).

Each of these later TV shows generated new box sets, but from the late 1990s into the 2000s, a parallel venture brought LEGO ever closer to a large-scale effort in moving-image production: the licensing of its brand to movie companies for box sets that derived from big studio blockbusters. While many LEGO box sets from the 1960s on had moved from the narratively neutral context of town or city building (which might or might not encourage story-making) to highly narrativized efforts to imagine environments (from land to sea to outer space) as backdrops for adventure and dramatic conflict (for example, knights versus knights—or dragons!—in a series of sets about the world of castles), these were never linked to specific movies and stood rather as in-house attempts by TLG to make its "System of Play" fit into a media landscape increasingly about franchisable stories. But in 1999, in its very first deal to license intellectual property with a media company, TLG paired with LucasFilm to bring out physical sets based

on *Star Wars* films. The sets were—and are—a gigantic success, and it would seem they brought into the LEGO branded
world even many of the film franchise's fans who came to it less
from interest in LEGO than in anything *Star Wars*–related.
(By 2005, eight of the top ten best-selling LEGO box sets were
from *Star Wars*.) Of course, *The LEGO Movie* itself has a great
in-joke reference to *Star Wars* when, stuck in the middle of the
ocean, Emmet and his gang realize the only thing that can get
them going again is a hard-to-find hyper-drive replacement
part. Suddenly *Star Wars'* Millennium Falcon, piloted by Han
Solo and Chewbacca, shows up, and Batman is able to steal the
needed part after pretending he is going off to party with the
Star Wars dudes. A coda later shows the Millennium Falcon
not being able to achieve hyper-speed because of the missing
component, and being swallowed up by a gigantic space animal, the Exogorth from *The Empire Strikes Back*.[8]

Can't have LEGO pieces go missing!

Interestingly, many of the Star Wars kits involved lots of
pieces for the "assembly required." In other words, they often
necessitated commitment and the labor of love. Fan interest
in the films predictably meant that the engaged builder would

tend to want to use all the pieces as proscribed so as to achieve constructions that resembled what was revered in the films: might not the joke about *Star Wars* in *The LEGO Movie* stand as an astute comment on the functional necessity of every piece in a LEGO *Star Wars* box (leave out the hyper-drive and it can all come crashing down)? The sets served, then, as a kind of pedagogy into LEGO building practices: not all Star Wars fans may have been adept LEGO constructors beforehand (nor wanted to be), but they had to become such in order to fashion the complex Star Wars models TLG was offering them. (In contrast, when TLG brought out a "Galidor" line of box sets in 2002, based on a Fox Kids TV show that had had a one-year run, there just was not a large enough fan base from the series to make the spin-off work. And, conversely, LEGO fans complained because the sets—maybe because they derived from a show *for kids*—minimized the number of pieces required, unlike the complexity of many Star Wars kits.)

The first significant venture in stand-alone moving-image narrative for LEGO figures came in 2003 with a direct-to-DVD offering, *Bionicle: The Mask of Light* (with follow-ups), from the Bionicle series of minifigs: here, the characters have some of the constructed look of the figurines they derive from, but they also move and articulate in ways that real Bionicles couldn't (for example, the movie's Bionicles can open and close their fully-fingered hands). At a moment when many new product lines were crashing and burning for LEGO (most historians of the company say it over-extended itself in this period and got away from the core idea of the brick too often), Bionicle was a tremendous *multimedia* success: centering on HR Giger-like creatures (with angular joints, pointed protrusions, fierce looks, sharp weapons, and so on) that substituted ball-and-joint connection for the traditional LEGO stud-and-tube, Bionicle moved between comics, TV shows, direct-to-video offerings, webcasts, stop-motion, and live-action animation, offering an ever-expanding narrative world that one could consume in multiple media forms, the stories available in each reinforcing and extending each other.

At virtually the same moment (the beginning of the 2000s), a unique (and maybe curious) LEGO venture into moving images appeared. In 2000, TLG created a new line of sets called LEGO Studio and for the first offering partnered with Steven Spielberg to host Steven Spielberg Moviemaker, with 433 pieces. Moviemaker (as we will henceforth call it) imagines a movie set inspired by Spielberg's Jurassic Park series (two installments of which had come out by then), with a roaring dinosaur and human minifigs fleeing in a roadster, and with some movable parts to the decor (a floor that slid open to reveal a lava flow, walls that broke apart to indicate the ensuing disaster). Unlike other movie-inspired kits (including Star Wars offerings from the previous year onward), Moviemaker also notably included pieces that clearly established this as a movie set, such as klieg lights, cameras, clapboards, and even a complex tracking-and-panning mechanism that a camera could be mounted on, as well as minifigs that made up a movie crew including, strikingly, a bearded figure who was supposed to represent Spielberg himself and was provided with a megaphone so that he could shout out movie directions. (Amusingly, the 2011 television special, *LEGO Star Wars: The Padawan Menace* includes a minifig of Spielberg's blockbuster buddy George Lucas, who has to keep stepping into the frame when Darth Vader, who actually is not supposed to be in the film, persists in coming on set and interrupting the action.)

LEGO, camera, action!

The biggest innovation of Moviemaker was the inclusion of a digital camera (in plastic with LEGO-like colors) and PC software it could interface with so that consumers might consider making their own action films with the decor and minifigs and props. The camera offered, among other functions, options for varied transitions from scene to scene (from wipes to fades to dissolves); a sound effects library (for example, dinosaur roars); a music library (generic open-domain songs plus multiple styles they could be played in); microphone input for dialogue and narration; and titling in multiple fonts and formats. The camera provided both stop-motion frame-by-frame animation and live-action (for the latter, the physical pieces included a series of thin poles to be kept, hopefully, out of camera range in order to move figurines physically around on the set). There had already been a tradition of amateur-made LEGO films—known under the name "brick films" (or "brickfilms")—and multiple internet sites had sprung up to show off these home creations. Now, with its own proprietary camera and software, TLG was centralizing and normalizing LEGO filmmaking as a corporate-directed creative activity logically connected to other play activities of the LEGO fan (such as building physical constructions and manipulating characters within them in made-up stories). Notably, the Moviemaker camera included a button that could link the home filmmaker to the LEGO website, and it also enabled sending of productions by email to friends and fans around the world. In this way, Moviemaker sought to bring the brick-film tradition into its orbit, both in terms of profits from the original purchase of the set and a degree of potential ownership of, or at least sharing of, footage shot by the amateurs (who presumably would be quite proud to imagine that their works were worthy of being uploaded to LEGO and perhaps seen by Spielberg himself).

More than just providing visual instructions on how to build the figures and environments in the set—although it did do that too—the manual that came with Moviemaker included a basic primer, framed ostensibly in the first-person voice of Spielberg himself, in narrative moviemaking. There was pedagogy about stories being based on conflict; about continuity; about the relative roles of dialogue and resonant imagery; about the importance of well-planned preproduction (including storyboarding); about the function of camera angle and camera movement in contributing dramatic effect (for example, a track-in could reveal important narrative detail in suspenseful or impactful fashion); about mood lighting (including the use of filters); and, above all, about the importance of imagination in inspiring good storytelling and vital imagery.

Sets and accessories for LEGO Studio continued to appear on the market for three years, adding Indiana Jones and Spider-Man to the mix, along with more generic moviemaking components (camera, crews, lighting, and so on). Some of the kits included moving parts—such as a stuntman mini-set that involved a catapult and, most strikingly, Movie Backdrop

Studio, which featured a battery-operated scroll unfurling a cityscape in front of which a LEGO helicopter and a police car sped forward (propelled by a track that was just below the scroll's bottom so one could craft the shot without the track being visible).

In her manual on LEGO filmmaking, Sarah Herman asserts that to appeal to kids, and to make it less labor-intensive for them to craft animation frame-by-frame, TLG had set the camera's frame rate low (fifteen frames per second, below the standard rate for professional filmmaking) but suggests that this simplifying gesture may have made the camera less useful to Adult Fans of LEGO who wanted more sophistication to their efforts.[9] The camera disappeared from the later sets, although these still came with a CD, this time with clips of completed LEGO films to show off examples of what could be accomplished in LEGO moviemaking.

But a growing number of the movie box sets included *no* filmmaking equipment among the props and simply reproduced canonic scenes from films, allowing for creative effort (construction and narrative play) on the part of consumers that might have little or nothing to do with moviemaking per se. For example, in 2002 TLG brought out a series of sets based on classic Universal monster movies—*Dracula, Frankenstein, The Werewolf, The Mummy*—that referenced moments from those films but left out filmmaking props. (In this manner, the sets were similar to the vastly popular plastic models of Universal monsters that the Aurora company marketed in the 1960s: one could build monsters from movies, but as free-standing icons of horror seemingly independent of the act of filmmaking that originally had brought them into existence.)

The LEGO Studio line petered out as consumers increasingly had available to them personal devices (cell phones, etc.) that could enable them to make LEGO movies on the fly. And the inauguration of YouTube in the middle of the first decade of the 2000s made it much easier for amateurs to post films, independent of official LEGO channels.

By the time of *The LEGO Movie* in 2014, themed sets derived from movies—especially from iconic scenes in movies—had proliferated, but the idea of LEGO-directed filmmaking itself as something the fan could do had dropped out as an explicit part of the play. Intriguingly, though, *The LEGO Movie 2* returned to the original idea of Moviemaker by tying in to kits featuring film crew members and their equipment (lights, cameras, tracking set-ups), but updating the consumer's own possible moviemaking by including a downloadable app for mobile device, rather than a plastic digital camera.

So, by 2008, when Warner Bros. came a-courting with the idea of a feature film, The LEGO Group had been involved with moving images in myriad ways. The company didn't *need* to license its intellectual property to a *film* studio, but, with the right arrangement, it could stand to benefit: brand recognition could get a boost across media; the company would show its up-to-dateness by going beyond the physical brick to a renewed embrace of imagistic (especially digital) realms; and there was great possibility for tie-ins (games, books, theme park attractions, and so on). The company gave its blessing, and the work of animation—both preproduction and production—kicked into high gear.

Production History, Part 2:

The Animation Process

> Two Australian animators are having lunch.
> The eager, younger one states, "Animation is imagination!"
> His companion—older, more pragmatic—replies,
> "Yes, but is it local imagination or imported imagination?"
>
> —Australian animation joke from Keith Scott,
>   animation voicer and historian[1]

Under the supervision of directors Phil Lord and Chris Miller along with animation supervisor Chris McKay—but with lots of trustful delegation of technical and creative decisions— Australian-based animation and digital effects company Animal Logic handled the animation for *The LEGO Movie*.[2] McKay served as liaison and made a number of trips to Sydney, where Animal Logic was based. Essentially, he oversaw what Animal Logic would be contributing to the film. In fact, it had been anticipated that McKay, a veritable *codirector* on the film for his insight on the visuals, *would* officially be credited as such along with Lord and Miller, but the live-action material from the film's ending brought the film into conflict with Directors Guild of America rules about who could count as director for a live-action film, and that organization did not credit McKay for his clear directorial contribution.

Nicely, though, he would soon be handed full directorial rein for *The LEGO Batman Movie*, and there he got appropriate credit (the film is fully a work of animation with no interfering live-action).

Dan Lin and Lord and Miller made trips to Sydney as well, but McKay seems to have been the point person, as he had expertise in the look of stop-motion animation from work on cult series like *Robot Chicken*. In an age of wide-bandwidth fast data transfer, however, much of the animation output went back and forth electronically, and geographic distance seems not to have been an issue in the making of the movie.[3]

Foreign producers, including in Hollywood, have looked to Australia as a site for production since the beginnings of cinema history. Outsourcing some or all of a film to Australia, or to other countries, can save on labor costs, aid in getting around quotas and tariffs, and help spend revenues that are blocked for export (for example, distribution fees accrued locally), along with offering other economic advantages. But Australia obviously has particular appeal for location shoots that take advantage of its landscape, both spectacular and, in its own way, desolate (a quality on display in Stanley Kramer's end-of-world parable, *On the Beach*).[4] For instance, Australian film scholar Adrian Danks chronicles how, in the latter half of the 1950s, the venerable but essentially moribund English production company Ealing tried desperately for one last gasp of vitality by moving some productions out of the enclosed and artificial space of the studio back home and into the open air of the Australian countryside.[5] And in 1960 Warner Bros. itself (the company, that is, that years later would make *The LEGO Movie* and its follow-ups) produced a lush middle-brow prestige film set in Australia, *The Sundowners*, which received five Academy Award nominations and was a sort of transposition of the American epic Western to Australia (here, it's a sheep drive and not a cattle drive), with *High Noon* director Fred Zinnemann at the helm and *High Noon* composer Dimitri Tiomkin contributing a rousing score.[6] Yet the story of Hollywood's turn to Australia increasingly mutates into an account of what happened when entertainment cinema became more effects-driven, and photographic reality (location shooting, for instance) came to take a back seat to digitalization.

Revealingly, as Keith Scott (who himself does voices for Australian animation) points out in his contribution on "Australia" to an encyclopedic history of animation, Hollywood had outsourced animation labor to Australia as early as the late 1950s, when several firms in the country took on the repetitive labor on backgrounds in TV cartoons for US production companies, which were hoping to save money while meeting the increasing demand for daytime cartoons. In 1970, one of the Sydney-based companies received a contract from the famed American animation studio Hanna-Barbera to do work on a cartoon series: William Hanna himself made a trip to Sydney to oversee the process, and this led to his company setting up its own branch there (H-B Australia)—and dealing with legal action (in which they were victorious) by local animation businesses claiming that H-B was poaching talent.[7]

In 1988, Warner Bros. partnered with its Australian distributor Village Roadshow (which had started as a chain of Australian drive-ins before entering the distribution arena) to buy the failed Brisbane studio of legendary producer Dino De Laurentiis, who had found success in the past in moving production away from Hollywood, yet fell on hard times in the economically volatile 1980s.[8] But when film director Alex Proyas, who had grown up in Sydney and attended film school there, decided to return to Australia for his effects-heavy science-fiction feature *Dark City*, produced by Warner subsidiary New Line, the production settled down in Sydney and not at Warner/Village Roadshow. Sydney had been trying to entice runaway production by providing a rentable production facility owned by 20th Century Fox, part of an entertainment complex with a fairground next door to studio facilities. *Dark City* was filmed at these locations and at other venues in the area, and as it relied largely on special effects, the production also drew heavily on the contributions of effects companies in the city.[9]

The striking visuals of *Dark City* and its subsequent cult success convinced Warner Bros. to choose Sydney for its bigger-budget SF *Matrix* trilogy, and the studio turned to multiple effects firms in the city, including Animal Logic, for the film's vast array of digital effects. Founded in 1991 by Zareh Nalbandian and Chris Godfrey, Animal Logic had been working on effects in commercials and television shows along with feature film titling and moment-to-moment effects in live-action films that weren't overwhelmingly or ostentatiously effects-driven, such as *The Thin Red Line* and the *Babe* films (from Australian-born director George Miller).

The visual effects for *The Matrix*, shared among a number of Sydney digital companies, won the Oscar in that category, and this helped solidify Animal Logic's reputation. Another boost came in 2003 when acclaimed Chinese director Zhang Yimou elected to shoot the martial arts film *Hero* in Sydney, in very large part because of the notoriety of Animal Logic in the effects field (some of the TV commercials Animal Logic had been involved in were for Asian television markets and had gotten the company known in that region of the world). Zhang would later return to Sydney to shoot *House of Flying Daggers*, with Animal Logic in charge of effects once again. Interestingly, the very fact that Animal Logic's efforts could work so well for non-Hollywood films (but ones using the action genre to open up to global markets like the US) may well have amplified its attractiveness as an effects house to *Hollywood* studios: it was showing off its versatility with regard to any assignment thrown its way, an attractive quality in times demanding flexibility and inventiveness in effects work. By the 2000s, Nalbandian was reporting that up to 90 percent of Animal Logic's work was for foreign production companies. As significant a figure, perhaps, was Nalbandian's additional estimate that 10 percent of every revenue dollar was being channeled back into research and development, an important process for an independent effects company that needed to signal it was constantly innovating and constantly open to the new effects needs of the foreign production companies.[10] Effects work is a notoriously volatile part of the movie business, with companies working piecemeal from project to project and often undercutting their profits by underbidding their services, and Nalbandian seems well aware of the struggles to keep afloat.[11]

Revealingly, an alliance of government, tourist board, business (including real estate), and cinema professionals at the national level have in recent years given special recognition to the recruitment of *digital* production from abroad, seeming then to admit that Australia is now attractive not only for live-action location filmmaking of a sort that would show off the land, but also for a technical proficiency in crafting fantasy images tied to no location and thereby fostering a global look and a global appeal. In particular, a film such as *The LEGO Movie* benefited from a very generous government-sponsored rebate program specifically targeted at digital production organized from overseas: the so-called PDV Offset (Post [-Production], Digital, Visual Effects), administered by Screen Australia, gives back up to 30 percent of its expenditure to any digital production budgeted at over $15 million and made in Australia. Notably, there is a rebate for live-action, but it is only half that of the PDV, as if to confirm where priorities now lie in an increasingly digitalized world of images. (As of this writing, though, there are some initiatives to increase the live-action rebate to the same percentage as the PDV; Animal Logic, which often crafts digital effects *for live-action films*, has been one strong proponent of the change.) *The LEGO Movie* is often singled out in promotional materials by Screen Australia and other government and business bodies as a key case of the success of the PDV rebate. Indeed, the very page on the Screen Australia website that introduces production off-sets features, as its sole image, Batman, Emmet, and Wyldstyle from the film, as if to confirm just how much *The LEGO Movie* did to represent Australia as an attractive production venue.[12]

In 2006, after continuing to contribute effects to a number of live-action films such as *Hero*, including Hollywood films that centrally relied on Australian directors (such as Baz Luhrmann for *Moulin Rouge*), Animal Logic got its first assignment for the entirety of animation on a feature film, *Happy Feet*, directed by George Miller for Village Roadshow with distribution by Warner Bros. *Happy Feet* won the Oscar for Best Animated Feature, a surefire sign that Animal Logic

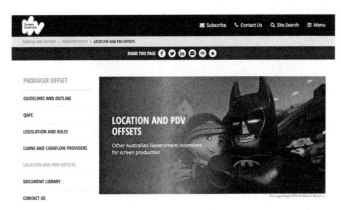

The LEGO brand helps brand Australia

had become a major player in the field. While one should be
wary of assuming there is a "house style" for a company whose
very endurance no doubt relies to a great degree on flexibility—
the need to vary stylistic outputs according to the demands
of this or that client—we can find in *Happy Feet* some of the
visual virtuosities that have made Animal Logic a go-to firm
in today's animation orbit and that later would be used in *The
LEGO Movie*. *Happy Feet* exhibits a firm grasp of the animation of non-human beings (penguins and other animals of the
north); it demonstrates great mastery of exhilarating forward
camera movement (as well as the camera swirling around
characters); it shows powerful richness in the depiction of the
elements (clouds in the sky, underwater, ice floes, and so on)
and the thrusting movement of characters through them; it is
quite adept in the rendering of crowds and mass assemblages
(yet with a variety of individualized movements so that not
every creature is in absolute unison with every other one); and

The digital rendering of natural elements: The LEGO Movie's *ocean*

it is quite proficient in crafting digital lighting effects that contribute to both realistic motivation and drama.

Nalbandian became executive producer on Animal Logic's next animated feature, *Legend of the Guardians*, once again for Warner Bros. *Legend* is a film of sumptuous animation, but two visual qualities that might link it to *The LEGO Movie*, where they are also used to great effect—namely, a driving forward motion (so central to *The LEGO Movie*, as emphasized earlier) and transitions into slow motion during action sequences—may not signal "house style" so much as stand as confirmation of Animal Logic's capacious ability to meet client needs (in other respects, the two films do not look much alike at all). Specifically, *Legend* was directed by action director Zack Snyder, for whom the dynamic rush of the camera and slow motion as opponents clash had become veritable trademarks in films like *300*. With *Legend*, Animal Logic confirmed its versatility and its grasp of the need for fantasy to develop striking styles all its own. It was on the basis of Animal Logic's perfection of animation for *Legend* that the film's executive producer, Chris DeFaria, recommended the company to the Warner Animation Group for *The LEGO Movie*.

Animation, of course, as argued earlier, severs any direct connection between the real world and the filmic one. For Hollywood to outsource feature animation to a city like Sydney clearly has nothing to do with the aesthetics of location, as had been the case in earlier Hollywood live-action movies filmed down under. Indeed, in recent decades there have been numerous animated features that in their very narratives are all about disconnecting fantasy locations on-screen from any real-world counterpart as a way of globalizing subject matter and extending its appeal (a striking example is *Big Hero 6*, whose key locale is a mash-up of Tokyo and San Francisco).[13] While *The LEGO Movie* nominally seems set in its first scenes in a US city, it's a decidedly generic image of the urban with very little that signals Americanness as a specific way of life. Even when the narrative leaves the city behind for an action-filled sojourn in the "Old West," it is easy to view this as an Old West of the imagination, a mythic space available to many cultures worldwide that have grown up on the form. (In fact, the West here is channeled at least partly through the European revisions of the movie genre, especially in the Italian Westerns of the 1960s. Lord and Miller even employed, for a specific sound effect, an Italian craftsman who had worked with Ennio Morricone on the distinctive sound for Sergio Leone movies.)

More generally, *The LEGO Movie* exhibits a spatial rootlessness, running through multiple geographies and ultimately de-realizing many of them, that perhaps itself serves as an allegory for globalization's push beyond fixed boundaries: certainly, the fact that President Business changes his moniker to Lord Business seems to indicate an expansive placelessness bound to no one nation. The advantages of outsourcing in such a case, then, have more to do with economics, labor,

Once upon a time in the LEGO West

and technical prowess than any attempt to represent physical locale. (It is worth noting that the success of *The LEGO Movie* enabled Animal Logic itself to globalize and open a branch production facility in Vancouver, Canada, much closer to Los Angeles than Sydney, and it was there that *The LEGO Movie 2* was made.)

The LEGO Movie was preceded three years earlier at Animal Logic by a LEGO short animation, *Star Wars: The Padawan Menace*, a veritable test run for the subsequent feature film with Zareh Nalbandian as one of the executive producers. A twenty-two-minute television special with a strong afterlife on DVD, *Padawan Menace* does anticipate *The LEGO Movie* in some respects (one has to wonder, though, if the three times this or that character in the short film describes something as "awesome" is coincidental to the feature film's "Everything Is Awesome" hit song). For instance, the short involves numerous scenes of LEGO construction and deconstruction, including animated minifig characters coming apart and being reduced to their base component. As in *The LEGO Movie*, characters don't so much die as break into pieces, and often continue talking, as if to suggest they never really gave up the ghost—pun intended in the case of Vitruvius in *The LEGO Movie*, who indeed returns from decapitation as a specter. (In an amusing in-joke, one of the characters to be dismantled most violently in *Padawan Menace* is Jar Jar Binks, famously hated by many viewers of *The Phantom Menace* feature film.) The emphasis on deconstruction, rather than destruction, is in keeping with the LEGO philosophy about play (for the longest time, the company wanted to avoid violence and death within its box sets) and offers a comment on the durability of the LEGO brick itself: it is seemingly indestructible, and once a construction is disassembled, the brick is still available to serve as a core for a new creation. If both *Padawan Menace* and *The LEGO Movie* offer recurrent scenes of things—minifigs, but also their habitations and their vehicles—being taken apart and returned to the original state of random pieces, they are also about rebuilding and constructing anew, luxuriating in the creative potential that LEGO enable.

Yet *Padawan Menace* does not manifest all the craft and tricks that made *The LEGO Movie* seem so visually unique just a few years later. Despite some moments of in-joke self-reflexivity that remind viewers that the fiction they are watching is indeed a fiction, a made-up construction itself, *Padawan Menace* does not adopt the feature film's conceit that its characters actually exist as inanimate toys outside the fiction. Thus, the minifigs in *Padawan Menace* aren't required to bear all of the limitations of real-world LEGO minifigs: most notably, their clasp hands can open and close, something unavailable to the minifigs of *The LEGO Movie* according to the conceit of that film. And in *Padawan Menace* the environments the minifigs move through are not made up of LEGO pieces; they are presented as realistic (if somewhat flat in look) backdrops to the fictional action of the characters.

To whatever extent *Padawan Menace* serves as a test run for LEGO film narrative, production at Animal Logic on *The LEGO Movie* itself took over two years, with upwards of several hundred people working on the project at certain moments. From the start, it seems, Warner Bros. had planned to give the film a stop-motion look, but done digitally, since actual brick animation would have been too time-consuming and too costly, especially once it was decided to make everything in the LEGO world on-screen—from buildings to oceans to effects like explosions—be composed of LEGO bricks. Some executives were skeptical that digital animation made to look like stop-motion could work, but Warner Animation Group and Animal Logic crafted an "audition" reel with a digital but physical-seeming Emmet going through a range of emotions (and actually talking to the viewer as if he were indeed in an audition) in a manner that showed he could resonate emotionally. As Phil Lord and Chris Miller explained to me in a phone conversation, it was important to demonstrate that digital simulation of frame-by-frame animation could work visually, that LEGO minifigs could show emotion, and especially that they could do so even as their dramatization adhered to strict rules about solidity and nonpliability. It was important to the team that, unlike in earlier LEGO ventures for television and direct-to-DVD, the feature-film LEGO characters be bound to the same laws of fixity and limited articulation that LEGO minifigs have in the real world (no arm bending here!).

Fxguide.com, a rigorous website devoted to the effects industry and its technologies, offers a very informative half-hour video interview filmed at Animal Logic with three key members of the team for *The LEGO Movie*, complemented by an essay that puts many of the points into discursive form.[14] The material presented has loads of technical detail to satisfy the geeks, but there are also important broader lessons around Animal Logic's approach to animation for *The LEGO Movie*. For instance, in light of the possible distinction between *playing* with LEGO and *watching* a LEGO movie, discussed earlier, it's revealing that one team member, Aidan Sarsfield (computer graphics supervisor for the film), talks in the video about how the *making* of the movie was like *playing* with LEGO—how, for instance, individual animators were allowed the freedom to invent background minifigs out of digitized bricks, just like a kid might custom-build a physical minifig. There is a revealing displacement here by which it's the personnel behind the movie (rather than, say, the spectators) who get to play and invent and engage with the creative potential so central to fundamental LEGO philosophy. Confirming their hearty enjoyment of the production process, the fxguide video shows men who really have had fun with their work and continue to have fun explaining it; this is fully a mark of membership in the Creative Class (to pick up urban theorist Richard Florida's famous term), geared not only to crafting diversion for others (we the audience) but to making entertainment of the sort that they themselves would enjoy just as much. (It's perhaps revealing in this respect how often creative personnel working on today's digitalized entertainment cite their children as a source not only of inspiration but also of useful input. Obviously, The LEGO Group itself also relies to a large degree on an image of LEGO as a creative force that endures over generations. For today's creative class, the assumption is that one never gets too old to appreciate the sheer fun of play, even within the seeming world of adult labor. This is a lesson that the father in *The LEGO Movie* has to learn bit by bit.)[15]

Another revealing aspect of the video interview is when Animal Logic production designer Grant Freckelton discusses how the very fact that the movie was about small-scale figurines who ultimately were just toys led to a design that—paradoxically, perhaps, but deliberately—crafted its worlds and the narrative that transpired within them in dramatically large-scale ways. The idea was that the small LEGO world would get big-time treatment. As Freckelton explains, the chases, for instance, would be bigger and louder and more explosive, as if to provide an epic rendition of an essentially miniaturized premise. (Elsewhere on the web, in additional production history about *The LEGO Movie*, another crew member notes that the film was digitally shot in widescreen and with elaborate lighting effects to impart additional levels of importance to seemingly small subject matter.)[16]

Freckelton even notes that directors Phil Lord and Chris Miller came up with a term to describe this blend of big treatment with the little world of LEGO: "dumpressive," which is intended to capture the fact that the subject matter could essentially be seen as small and therefore silly or *dumb* (an action movie about LEGO minifigs!?!)—and remains, as we've seen, silly for some moviegoers who disdain the trend toward animated features in the mainstream of Hollywood moviemaking—yet be granted impressive visual treatment. Freckelton cites as a key example the scene in which Vitruvius, accompanied by Wyldstyle, takes Emmet on a journey inside the latter's mind: in a visual rendition borrowed from *The Matrix*, we see nothing but a field of white LEGO strips stretching into seeming infinity. That the mind, even in this case the fairly unassuming one of a fairly unassuming protagonist, would be made up of LEGO is a funny, because "dumb," gag, but the visual rendition—the screen becoming a vast expanse of LEGO extending everywhere—is "impressive."

Being and Nuttiness: big concepts and little figures

The LEGO Movie clearly and strikingly takes the conceit of a built fiction to its extreme: everything is LEGO and acknowledged as such for the viewer (for example, the LEGO ocean, one of the most striking effects in the film). In the early 2000s, TLG itself had developed an open-access computer program, LEGO Digital Designer (LDD), that fans could use to call up any and all LEGO pieces virtually, examine them from all angles, and then imagine building them into ever-more complex constructions. TLG worked with Animal Logic to customize the program and enable it to catalogue the many bricks it would need to visualize in three dimensions on-screen (two thousand different bricks, altogether). One feature that Animal Logic crafted was a program to offer shading and variation for *each* brick. For the animation of these bricks, a program was developed that added a wee bit of jitter, so as to approximate the jerkiness of stop-motion animation. (An additional effort was made to blur moving bricks slightly to create an effect so necessary to the effective visualization of motion.) Another program, developed for the film at Animal Logic, was LEGOscape, which would take mesh-like drawings of large environments for the film, such as the Wild West mesas and canyons, and fill the meshes up with bricks. It had also been decided to give the bricks a look of wear and tear, so the shading program was also made to include "numerous texture variations for each brick."[17] As several members of the Animal Logic team explain in a technical report, the rendering of the bricks on-screen (and this is before the additional work of simulating lighting on them) involved three steps, starting with the LEGO Digital Designer collation of pieces: "There were 3 layers to the surfacing of models—an automatic assignment of colors, transparency, and other visual properties from the LDD models; a semi-procedural level of per-brick surfacing to provide detail such as scratches, wear and tear, decals, etc.; and a 'model' level to add grunge and oxidation effects."[18]

Many fans of *The LEGO Movie*, along with its makers themselves, were taken aback when the movie did not receive an Oscar nomination in 2015 for the previous year's "Best Animated Feature." For what it's worth, the nominees were *Big Hero 6*, *The Boxtrolls*, *How to Train Your Dragon 2*, *Song of the Sea*, and *The Tale of the Princess Kaguya*, with *Big Hero 6* ultimately the winner. There was some speculation that the digital animation of the LEGO was so convincing that it was hard for some voters to actually accept it as animation and not something approximating to live-action, and speculation, too, that this example of a digital film trying to emulate a photographic look had spurred detractors, for whom photographic cinema was a sacred realm, not to be toyed with by animation pretending to look photographically real. Codirector Phil Lord, however, offered an inspired response to the Academy on Twitter, asserting, "It's okay. Made my own!," accompanied by the image of a LEGO Oscar all in golden pieces. As was often the case with *The LEGO Movie*, savvy snark was its own best reward.

MOC/Mock Oscar

Production History, Part 3:

The Screenwriter-Directors

"Our whole career seems like an extended dare."
　—*The LEGO Movie* cowriter and
　　codirector Chris Miller[1]

The "commentary" tracks to the television shows and films of Phil Lord and Chris Miller are often given over to raucous laugh riots (hence, not always to direct commentary) rich in ecstatic appreciation ("awesome!") of great moments from their works. These are guys—and it's important to acknowledge the guy qualities on display—who take justifiable pride in their comic astuteness and who easily, infectiously draw others into their orbit (not only those listening to the track, but also their guests, generally actors from the shows or films who then get caught up in the fun).[2] Lord and Miller's sheer enthusiasm for wry entertainment cinema with snarky attitude has made the writing/directing pair figures of cult veneration for fans of fantasy, animation, and action with a self-aware edge. And the self-awareness can extend, notably, to their own image: as noted, the Extra Features on the DVD for *The LEGO Movie* include a hilarious promotional campaign that imagines Lord and Miller in LEGO form themselves, directing line readings of the key actors but with Lord Business trying to take over their effort and insulting them for their lack of talent at comedy and (Phil Lord) for physical unattractiveness. Through such self-deprecation, Lord and Miller come across as endearing dudes. In keeping with the ironic twists that never settle down in *The LEGO Movie* (and, indeed, throughout their work), Lord and Miller seem simultaneously aware of male entitlement and intent to undercut it with savvy self-awareness (which can, as often happens in guy culture at large, itself twist into somewhat of an affirmation of the very qualities being disavowed). A small anecdote: when I mentioned to the owner of my local comics store that I would be writing on *The LEGO Movie*, he immediately and enthusiastically said simply, "Phil Lord and Chris Miller!," capturing their iconic status in today's media landscape.

Guys buddying up (22 Jump Street)

Yet for all the name recognition that Lord and Miller enjoy, I hesitate to treat them as auteurs—at least in the classic film studies sense of filmmakers who impart an irreducible personal vision to the form and content of their works. My hesitation, however, is not about denigrating them for falling short of some special mark (I am not saying they fail at being auteurs while others succeed), but derives rather from an intuition about how filmmakers function as executive creators in today's media environment. (It is important, in this respect, to note that Lord and Miller clearly often serve as hands-on producers as well as directors, and seem thereby to be creative facilitators of projects as much as "authors" of them.) It is tempting in using the concept of the auteur to assume this somehow makes a director transcend his (or her, but classically "his") times and bear a critical relationship to them. (This certainly was the case in the cinema studies take on seventies directors like Martin Scorsese or Stanley Kubrick or Robert Altman.) But it makes more sense to understand the work of direction as part of an industry process, rather than an aesthetic innovation standing above it.

To take just one example, many of Lord and Miller's offerings center on awkward and unassuming guys (sometimes paired with or contrasted to, or paired with *and* contrasted to, he-men types) who try to make a go of it in, and do in fact sometimes flourish in, environments that today have become fruitful for geeks and nerds who in previous macho times lacked charismatic virility. There is, for instance, the dweeby protagonist (played to type by Will Forte) of the well-named, post-apocalyptic TV series *Last Man on Earth*, who finds that survival as perhaps the only man around makes him necessarily desirable to the last women around; there is the protagonist of *Clone High*, "Abe Lincoln" (voiced by Forte), who, despite being replicated from his strong-willed namesake, is wishy-washy, conflicted, easily led astray, physically inadequate, and so on; and there's the seeming misfit Schmidt (Jonah Hill) in the *Jump Street* films, who discovers possibility in a geeky world where awkward misfits are now legitimated.

Emmet, in *The LEGO Movie*, is perhaps a little different from the stereotypical once-upon-a-time nerdy misfit: he's so bereft of defining qualities that he doesn't even rise to the level of dweeb or nerd. Off the radar of those around him, he is still the loser who goes unnoticed and unappreciated until he can assume the title of hero through both brain and a bit of brawn.

The point, though, is that this stereotype of the loser who has to rise to the occasion has widespread currency in our culture (and is often one way, perhaps, for guys to render themselves seductive in an age that often has little time for older-style machismo), and it may be as much the case that Lord and Miller, clearly savvy about patterns in our popular culture (so that, to take a telling example, the *Jump Street* films include an "angry black captain" who comments himself on the omnipresence of this stereotype so promulgated in film and television), tap astutely into tropes and motifs of the time, rather than in any way originate them or "author" them. Broadly, for instance, the dweeb who turns out to be a hero in his own manner fits well into the realm of "the Creative Class"—made up of geeky information workers who are now admired (intellectually but also, importantly, emotionally and even romantically) for accomplishments not of physical prowess but of intellect, information, and cultural creativity.[3] In a cinephilic appreciation of cult movies, Phil Lord shows, for instance, awareness of how the dweeb stereotype permeates culture at large: "I'm certainly not the only filmmaker who insistently writes awkward characters who want something that they are incapable of getting—the person whose ambition

exceeds their ability is a really endearing character and is
repeated again and again—but it's certainly something that
I've been interested in."[4]

To be sure, there are motifs that run through Lord's and
Miller's work and provide it with a somewhat distinctive style.
For example, they are quite enamored of frenetic montages
filled with wacky images to capture moments of intense
trauma, psychological disarray, or even (sometimes drug-
induced) hallucination (one episode of their TV series *Clone
High* is a veritable parody from beginning to end of psyche-
delic tripping—and of classic cinematic renditions of drug experiences). And if such montages offer a dynamic compacting
of time (as when Emmet in *The LEGO Movie* has a fall that
leads to an explosion of images that condense memories and
visions he's had earlier), Lord and Miller also seem quite in-
vested in the converse to sped-up time: specifically, their films
luxuriate in distended temporality, a slowing down of time's
passage to a crawl: people stuck in stultifying routines at work
(for example, Schmidt and Jenko in *21 Jump Street* tooling
around ever so slowly on silly-looking mini-bikes on their seemingly dead-end and, for a long time, uneventful first assignment as park cops; Emmet announcing to his coworkers
dancing along with him that he could listen to "Everything Is
Awesome" for hours while a title announces "5 Hours Later"
and we see everyone still grooving to the beat) and even at rest
(Emmet sitting alone on his couch to enjoy free time; Batman
in *The LEGO Batman Movie* watching his Lobster Thermidor
microwave in real time) or just at life per se (one dilemma for
the titular protagonist of the TV series *Last Man on Earth* is
how to fill up time, moment after excruciating moment). Another version of temporal stretching comes in slow reaction

by this or that character to something someone else has said or done—usually something inane or improbable: Lord and Miller's films, both live-action and animated, are replete with long pauses that fix on a character as he or she reacts (although that's maybe too active a word for the studied impassivity of the response) to the nonsense he/she seemingly has to put up with.[5]

The implacable yet often scornful, quiet calm with which Lord and Miller's protagonists take in, ever so slowly, the seeming inanities of those around them connects to another quality of their films, one that is a bit harder to put into precise language. Quite simply, they are great directors of actors' performance—evident here in the sort of studied impassivity that slow reaction entails but also in the endless perfection of line delivery. Lord and Miller seem to bring out the best in their actors: to take the example of the *Jump Street* films, one easily appreciates the sarcasm of Ice Cube, the cocky blockheadedness of Channing Tatum, and the self-deprecations but also emotionalism of Jonah Hill (a brilliant performance probably not given its due because it's in an ostensibly tacky remake of a TV series, but made all the more striking by the overt sententiousness with which Hill handles the often deliberately silly material [this being another trait of Lord and Miller's films: seriousness in the midst of zany comedy]). It is worth noting in passing how often Lord and Miller enlist cast members and regular guests from *Saturday Night Live*, such as Will Ferrell and Maya Rudolph, in their movies (on the *Cloudy with a Chance of Meatballs* DVD commentary track, they brag about nine members of the SNL cast appearing in the film): these actors bring to their roles all the connotations of in-joke mass culture, a satiric and even snarky awareness of the popular culture that surrounds us and the powers of comedy in affectionately mocking it.[6]

Lord and Miller met as undergraduates at Dartmouth in the late 1990s and evidently hit it off right away. Miller double majored in government and studio art, and Lord was an art history major (and had a background in painting). They seem to have spent endless hours in the art studios working on projects. They took several film production classes, including a first-year one in animation (taught by famed animator David Ehrlich) that, it seems, introduced them to bare-bones cartooning, a talent that would come into play in the deliberately retro and stripped-down look of their much-revered animated TV series *Clone High*, and be integral to the mix of styles (including odes to hand-drawn "on the twos" superflat animation) in their *Spider-Man: Into the Spider-Verse*.

Lord's first big animation project, "Man Bites Breakfast," was about a breakfast cereal box from the point of view of the cereal inside. David Ehrlich noted in an email to me how such an effort helped Lord craft a visual dynamic that would viscerally engage the spectator: "Phil had a strong intuitive sense of physical perspective changes that grew into a sensitive perception of dramatic transitions that could keep the viewer involved. Simply put, whenever he saw rushes that bored HIM, he knew there had to be some sort of dramatic shift."

Film professor Mark Williams, who got to know both of them and had Phil Lord in a cotaught course, Japanese Literature and Cinema: Gender and Nationalism, recounted to me just how energizing a presence they were on campus. In his words, it was easy to "register the dynamism of their own creative efforts," and he suggests that the bare-bones approach they would have started with in animation (frame-by-frame, often of hand-drawn material) undoubtedly helped cement their working relationship, as the labor-intensity of such animation is mitigated somewhat by collaborators sharing and working well together and establishing their own division of labor. (One Dartmouth professor suggested that one of the pair seemed more a "soulful searcher" than his teammate, and this may have allowed for that strikingly effective emotional core that often shows up in Lord-Miller works—for example, the heartfelt sentiment to family interaction in *Spider-Man: Into the Spider-Verse*—even as these works also exhibit irony and jokiness to undercut the sentimentality.)

Team effort led to an important side venture that seems to have honed Lord and Miller's talents as illustrators and sardonic wits. Specifically, Miller revived the campus humor magazine *Jack-O-Lantern* and staffed it with Lord and other animation students increasingly drawn into their orbit. As David Ehrlich recalls, "The writing and graphics mocked student, faculty, and administration pretentions." Miller's animation project was a very sardonic parody of talk shows, "Sleazy the Wonder Squirrel," and he adapted that to a regular comic strip in the paper. The effort was not without controversy: for example, one installment of Sleazy criticized the level of care and diagnosis available at Dick's House, the campus medical center, and was roundly attacked by doctors and evidently led to intervention from the dean's office.[7]

For all the action-driven commercialism of their feature films, the Ivy League background may help explain some of the knowingness that floats over the seemingly uncritical embrace of popular form. Lord and Miller are adept at mixing silliness and sheer sensation with a savviness that means their films work at multiple levels and for multiple constituencies—not just parents and kids, as we see for *The LEGO Movie*, but also everyday audiences as well as college kids with education in diverse levels of mass and high culture. (To take just one example of the ways their films can split audiences, *22 Jump Street* opens with a montage that recaps significant moments from its predecessor *21 Jump Street*, but includes one faked scene *not in the original film*—Schmidt and Jenko in a kitchen trying awkwardly to boil lobsters together. On the DVD commentary track for *22*, Lord and Miller laughingly note how, when they showed the movie at Dartmouth, the "film students" easily got the reference to *Annie Hall*, while screenings elsewhere left viewers silent or bewildered at a scene they don't remember being in the first film.)

It's an important mark of Lord and Miller's own capacious ability to range across, and embrace, levels of culture from art cinema to lowbrow comedy, that the jokes in their films don't seem to assume the noncollege viewers are somehow less informed. One senses that the filmmakers appreciate different sorts of moviegoers finding something to match their levels of taste, whatever they are. As Lord and Miller put it on the commentary track for *Cloudy with a Chance of Meatballs*, when what they term a "gross-out kiss-barf" is immediately followed by Sam mentioning an amuse-bouche (with an ordinary citizen of the town wondering what that means), this is all about "high and low in the same place. That's the whole point." Their knowingness, and even irony sometimes, about the mechanisms and conventions of vast realms of popular culture does not preclude fanboy appreciation of that culture.

Lord and Miller can bring recondite references and ideas into their mass art. To take a minor example, the Cloud Cuckooland of *The LEGO Movie* derives from Aristophanes, an erudite allusion for its own sake. More ambitiously, their films and shows traffic, as do many works of popular culture today, in conceptual conundrums around identity, memory, temporality, etc. (I refer the reader back to my earlier discussion of the adult aspects to contemporary feature animation.) It is indeed significant to note how erudite, philosophic issues are now commonplace in supposedly escapist entertainment (*Avengers: Endgame*, for instance, relies centrally on time travel to resolve a major narrative dilemma, but importantly includes long dialogue scenes in which savvy characters debate what is and isn't possible in time travel).

The explicit awareness of—and explicit reflection on—philosophic questions is matched by equally savvy awareness in many such works of popular culture of the history of that popular culture itself. For many college students over recent decades (and perhaps many members of the general public as well), knowledge is not just about ideas out there (as in, for example, some abstract tradition of deep ideas), but in mass culture here and now, taught even in college classes. (A chase on the college campus in *22 Jump Street* passes by the building for the "Benjamin Hill Film School," a very knowing joke that links cinema education to the adolescent antics of the zanily lowbrow British comedian Benny Hill.)

For Lord and Miller, the grasp of popular culture means at a first level a concern with allusion and citation: for instance, a principal named Dadier in *21 Jump Street* is an homage to the teacher protagonist of the 1955 high school drama *The Blackboard Jungle* (interesting—and ironic—to imagine that he may have graduated to the fraught position of principal!). Beyond specific references peppered here and there through the films, there is broader recognition of stylistic trends in media and film history. In particular, in their animation, Lord and Miller range over cartoon history from the flat and angular modernism of 1950s UPA style for *Clone High*, to the nostalgia for stop-motion animation on display in *The LEGO Movie*, to the multiplicity of animation styles, older and newer, in the Lord-Miller production *Spider-Man: Into the Spider-Verse*. And they also show complex, ironic awareness not only of the aesthetics of film but also of the business—or, maybe we should say, of how the business is in many ways determinant of aesthetic choices. In particular, *21 Jump Street* bears a complex relationship to the TV show (one police commander explains to the protagonists that they're being assigned to a project that's a reboot of a 1980s effort despite lots of doubt that such a return to the past can work), while *22 Jump Street* goes so far as to mock its own status as a sequel (here, the "angry black captain" tells the protagonists that the powers-that-be think that by pouring twice as much money into the very same sort of operation as before, they will get twice the success— a very obvious reflection on the notion of the movie sequel itself, caught up in evident, but ever more money-draining, repetition).

In a story that sounds like Hollywood apocrypha but evidently happened, the son of Disney head Michael Eisner was an undergraduate at Dartmouth while Lord and Miller were there. He saw a profile of Miller in a local publication, *Dartmouth Life*, and brought it to his dad's attention. Eisner passed it around to Disney administrators, and it eventually ended up with Barry Blumberg, who was then head of Disney Television Animation and who took on the pair to develop script ideas for his unit. (As Phil Lord recounted to me in an email from August 21, 2019, Blumberg had telephoned Chris Miller at

Dartmouth and asked him to come for a meeting. Chris replied that he had college midterms coming up but was moving to Los Angeles over the summer and could come in then. He asked if he could bring Lord to the meeting, and it was quickly realized at Disney how the two worked as a team.)

Lord and Miller labored on a variety of projects while at Disney, but none immediately led to anything. One hilarious, surviving bit of work is a fake ad that was to run on Disney Saturday morning television for Brontë sister action figures: with the sort of tough-guy snarling narration that often accompanies action boy toy ads, we see Charlotte, Anne, and Emily getting rejected by the male literary establishment but then taking it on, first by throwing their books at the men (an obvious pun on the police notion of "throwing the book" at a guilty party), and then by uniting together as the composite action toy, the Brontësaurus![8]

While in college, Lord and Miller already had developed the premise for a television series, *Clone High*, which they went on to develop with coproducer Bill Lawrence, who had created *Spin City* and *Scrubs*. The series was picked up by MTV and coproduced with Touchstone Television, Disney's adult-targeted TV branch. It never had high ratings and sparked a major controversy (more on that in a moment), and was canceled after its first season. Yet it achieved major cult status and has legions of fans.

Just to recount the premise of *Clone High* is to capture much of its wackiness and irreverence. As part of a secret government project, scientists have made clones of famous figures from world history and put them all in a high school. Close to the mold of the historical figures they derive from are Cleopatra, a sexpot (but confused about what she wants from life),

and JFK, a womanizer (but without any of the liberal politics
that the real JFK was associated with). But other clones at the
high school don't always exhibit the same characteristics as
the luminaries they derive from: above all, protagonist Abe
Lincoln is a dweeby loser who is often conflicted about how
to move forward in his life. He is loved, though unrequitedly, by
Joan of Arc, whose very inability to feel the religious inspiration of her forebear has pushed her into a punky and de-
spairing Goth existence. Abe Lincoln's qualities of adolescent
inadequacy are shared with his sidekick Gandhi, who tries to
cover up for his shortcomings (striking out with women, for
instance) with a strutting jokiness that he imagines is cool but
just confirms to others what a loser he is. There were strong
calls for a boycott of the show by the Indian community, and
that seems to have played no small part in MTV's decision
to cancel *Clone High* after one season. Lord and Miller evidently tried to pitch additional seasons without Gandhi or with
Gandhi revealed to actually be someone else (child actor Gary
Coleman), but those ideas were rejected. Yet it may be that
Lord and Miller actually learned from the criticisms regarding
their handling of race in the series: the way they treat race
in both *The LEGO Movie*, vis-à-vis Morgan Freeman's Vitruvius, and especially *Spider-Man: Into the Spider-Verse* seems
much more user-friendly than the racialized humor of *Clone
High*, without losing any of the filmmakers' trademark comic
edge. While the former character (Vitruvius) is ironic and the
latter (Miles Morales) is deeply sincere, both approaches to
racialized identity seem more productively in tune with the
racial dynamics of the modern mediascape than that of the
earlier TV series.[9]

Shown on cable TV, *Clone High* exploits the freedom from FCC oversight that cable permits: it's a push-the-envelope series that trades in sexual innuendo, gross-out humor, bad taste (for example, the local diner the kids hang out at is called The Grassy Knoll and sports pictures of presidential assassinations on the wall), extreme gore, and an "equal opportunity" political incorrectness around race, sexuality, disability, and on and on (I call it "equal opportunity" since everyone and everything can get mocked: for example, JFK, with his mindless heterosexual machismo, is held up for ridicule, but so are his gay cross-dressing foster parents, buffoonish he-men merged into she-men).

Let the third episode of *Clone High*, "A.D.D. The Last 'D' Is for Disorder,'" stand as example. In the main plot line, Gandhi is diagnosed as having A.D.D. when he starts fidgeting too much in class. This occasions a song-and-dance number about A.D.D. (modeled on the "Telephone Hour" number in *Bye Bye Birdie*) in which high school kids start spreading rumors about the infectiousness of the illness and the debilities it will supposedly cause. Even Gandhi's best friend, Abe Lincoln, gives in to the prejudice when Cleo makes it clear that she doesn't want to be anywhere near Gandhi or anyone else who's near to him. But Abe learns about the dangers of prejudice (from comedian Tom Green in a wacky cameo) and rushes to the school's awareness fair, where he makes a speech for tolerance that everyone ignores, persisting instead in steadfast condemnation of Gandhi. Suddenly, impulsively, Abe realizes what he needs to do: he grabs Gandhi and gives him a long, deep kiss. In keeping with the series' deflation of high moralism and its luxuriating in political incorrectness and bad taste, everyone, unpredictably for what we expect of feel-good narrative turning points, is revolted by Abe's action, instead of converted to his cause, including Gandhi himself, who declares it "not cool." Yet as an unintended consequence, the townsfolk now empathize with Gandhi and redeem him while turning on Abe: as one citizen declares, "My discomfort with a man kissing another man is stronger than my hatred for people with A.D.D.," or as Cleo declares to Abe, "Your brave homoerotic gesture has changed my view about A.D.D. Just don't touch me."

As a bad-taste school comedy, *Clone High* seems very much to have been made in the spirit of the wildly successful *South Park* (itself a team effort—from the guy team of Trey Parker and Matt Stone), and Miller and Lord's later feature film works still draw from the anarchic, "equal opportunity" humor of that series, as well as their own, while also refining it substantially and decreasing the focus on shock value just for its own sake.

In a way, *Clone High* is all about taking the TV cartoons of the 1950s and updating them to more modern (or postmodern) times: the style is deliberately evocative of the modernist aesthetics in the cartoons that came from studios like UPA. As cartoon historian Amid Amidi has so well analyzed, this is a style based on hard edges and sharp lines, decentered compositions (often with extreme contrast between figures in the background and those in the foreground), backgrounds themselves rendered as solid but flat and blocky or blobby (often with nothing to distinguish walls from floors or ceilings), abstract settings, sharp angles, saturated colors, limited movement to characters, etc.[10]

Lord and Miller's first feature film was their very loose adaptation of the renowned 1978 children's graphic story by Judi

Updating animation to modern (or postmodern?) times

and Ron Barrett, *Cloudy with a Chance of Meatballs* (2009). As Sony was revving up its animation unit, *Clone High* production manager Geoff Suddleston recommended Lord and Miller, and they were brought in for one possible project, *Hotel Transylvania*. But the pair learned that Sony had acquired the rights to *Cloudy* and pushed enthusiastically to make this their debut film at the company.

Clocking in at under thirty pages, the original tale of *Cloudy* depicts a kindly granddad who, at their bedtime, tells his grandchildren of a wondrous town where weather descended onto the community as delectable comestibles, until the storms of food made the town dangerous and pushed the people to migrate to lands more like ours (where, for example, food was now available for purchase at supermarkets), but where they would feel a lingering nostalgia for a time of comfort food blanketing the land. Over a successive series of drafts—in what appears to have been a vexed preproduction process in which the team evidently was fired and rehired several times over—Lord and Miller pretty much abandoned the meager possibilities in the published story, except for a few visual motifs (like a pancake smothering the school or a Jell-O palace radiating out from the horizon). Instead, they fashioned a hero-redemption tale in which failed gadgeteer Flint Lockwood (voiced by Bill Hader, a regular Lord-Miller actor) comes up finally with a successful gizmo, a programmable invention shot off into outer space that can cause it to rain whatever food one desires. The gadget appears to be making the fortune of the town—which had fallen on hard times due to the relative distastefulness of the broad public toward its essential export, sardines—and giving it a worldwide reputation as a bountiful tourist destination, until the machine gets out of control and creates a bombarding storm that threatens to crush the entire world under the force of ever-mutating, ever-enlarging food items. Flint, aided by sidekicks who also need legitimation or redemption in one way or another, steps in to save the day.[11]

Fully of its cinematic moment in its emphasis on vibrant action sequences (for instance, Flint and buddies rush to the world's rescue in a fast flying vehicle) and a narrative of hero redemption, *Cloudy with a Chance of Meatballs* shows Lord and Miller reworking the classic children's tale to their own ends. It is, for instance, very savvy about contemporary mass culture and includes allusions to other popular culture: for example, it very clearly references disaster films and their common tropes (thus, after a montage of foods slamming down onto world monuments like Mount Rushmore and the Eiffel Tower and the British Houses of Parliament and the Great Wall of China, there is a cut to a newscaster who says the emergency is spreading everywhere after singling out monuments—a reference to the portentous attacks on the very same monuments that chronicle the disaster ramping up in films like *Armageddon*), with special attention to *Jaws* in its critique of a corrupt and rapacious mayor (voiced here by Bruce Campbell—another layer of popular culture reference, since he is a cult actor known to aficionados for his work in the *Evil Dead* films) who wants to cover over the ills besetting the seaport so as to not upset the tourist trade.

And the allusions can be even more recondite than that: as Lord and Miller explain on the commentary track, the very idea of a town gone into economic depression because of its reliance on a single industry (here, sardines) was inspired by Michael Moore's documentary *Roger and Me*, to the extent that the attempt by *Cloudy*'s evil mayor to exploit the failed commerce through a sardine-themed theme park reworks *Roger and Me*'s own depiction of Flint, Michigan's attempt to create a car theme park even as the car factory there is shutting down. Such references are arcane, scholarly, nerdy even. (Flint, of course, is the name, as well, of *Cloudy*'s protagonist.)

And of course, as noted, nerdiness or dweeby awkwardness as an outsider condition is a recurrent Lord-Miller theme, one played out to great effect in *Cloudy with a Chance of Meatballs*. From the first scene, where he fails in ignominious fashion at his first major invention, Flint is depicted as an outcast whose scientific ambition has in fact closed him off to many of the basic practices of everyday life (for example, we discover later on that he's never engaged in a snowball fight and doesn't really know how to do it). In degree of nerdiness, Flint is matched by love interest Samantha (nicknamed Sam)—who of course Flint doesn't initially know how to approach. Voiced by Anna Faris, Sam directly chronicles how she herself began as a self-declared nerd but then, anxious for acceptance, learned to hide her smarts beneath a cutesy, giggly exterior. But in a cultural moment where techno-smarts have become newly legitimated—the moment, as previously noted, of the "Creative Class"—Flint and Sam realize their science smarts are needed to defeat the food machine and, computer gear in hand, they set off into the skies, aided by onetime child star Baby Brent (voiced by Andy Samberg), who was the child mascot for the town's sardine company and who now also has an opportunity for heroic redemption. (In passing, it can be noted that the film's depiction of the evanescent childhood stardom of Baby Brent and his fall from celebrity offers another precise and canny example of Lord and Miller's capturing of the ins and outs of popular culture and popular media.)

Two aspects of Lord and Miller's quirky approach to mainstream filmmaking show up as early as the opening credits. First, since this is a film produced under the banner of Sony's Columbia Pictures subsidiary, we start, predictably, with the iconic logo of the so-called Columbia Lady, an upright figure in classical garb brandishing a torch, as if to offer (as it may have done for so many films over the years) a certain dash of cultural legitimacy. Yet immediately (and in keeping with the subsequent narrative of *Cloudy with a Chance of Meatballs*) she's ignominiously propelled off her imperious perch by a gigantic banana that flies down from the sky and knocks her to the ground. On the commentary track to *Cloudy*, Lord and Miller recount the many meetings they had to attend to convince Sony executives to agree to this bit of irreverence, yet it's one that clearly matters to them as they expanded on it in the opening to their film *Spider-Man: Into the Spider-Verse*, in which the Columbia Lady morphs between several different forms.

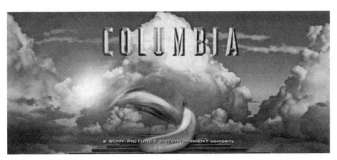

Columbia goes downright bananas

Second, and most interestingly, the credits include "A film by . . ." announcement, ever so typical of auteur films, but the phrase ends up completed by "a lot of people," a generous acknowledgment by Lord and Miller of the labor-intensive work of animation that is confirmed on their commentary track, where they endlessly note by name the specific contribution of this or that animator or other craftsperson on the film. Such open admission of the art of collaboration seems in keeping, indeed, with what I've argued is Lord and Miller's status not as special auteurs somehow standing above their culture but as savvy members of a creative community who share their craft—and craftiness—with so many others and who are all about facilitating and acknowledging creative work from every member of the crew.

For Columbia, Lord and Miller then wrote and directed the two films of the *Jump Street* franchise. Both possess a raunchiness and gross-out tone that the cable adventure *Clone High* had hinted at, and that seems worlds apart from the kid-friendlier feature animation (although the animated films do, as we see, have their edgy, out-there moments).[12] The *Jump Street* films show brazenly what one can have with an

R rating: sex and anatomical jokes, obscenity, political incorrectness, representation of drug culture, and on and on. When Lucy comments in *The LEGO Movie 2* that the apocalypse the DUPLO brought to Bricksburg made it a "heckish place to live in," the euphemism seems a kind of in-joke around what is permitted in an R-film (for example, "Crude and sexual content, pervasive language, drug material, teen drinking, and some violence," as the rating for *21 Jump Street* clarifies) in contrast to PG fare (*The LEGO Movie 2* is said, for instance, to have "Mild action and rude humor").

With their own production company, Lord Miller, Lord and Miller would take on assignments across media and at diverse studios without ever settling down at any one. This flexibility no doubt allows for a strong degree of creative freedom, but it also could make the team potentially vulnerable to the vagaries of those who hire them, a risk that was borne out in a controversial episode in Lord and Miller's directing career. In 2017 they were engaged by Disney to produce and direct a *Star Wars* spin-off prequel, *Solo*, but were fired four months into the shoot for what everyone on both sides of the disagreement officially termed "creative difference." Ron Howard was brought in to take over directing the film (evidently eventually reshooting more than 70 percent of Lord-Miller's material), while Lord and Miller retained "Executive Producer" mention in the credits (along with other listed executive producers). For what it's worth, the film, released in 2018, did only middling business compared to other efforts in the *Star Wars* franchise.

It is unclear what happened exactly, and it is probably impossible to know from the outside what the real story is. A claim repeated in the industry press (but originating from a single *Variety* article, so that its repetition may simply have to do with the availability of that one account rather than any deeper accuracy) maintains that Lord and Miller encouraged actors to engage in lots of improvisation around dialogue, and this may have even led to some deviation in plot development.[13] (It may also be that the improvisation slowed down the production schedule, something potentially worrisome for a labor-intensive, big-budget film.) Whatever the case, Lord and Miller were removed from the project. Their footage has never been shown publicly.

For all the problems of the *Solo* project, 2018 was also a year of triumph for Lord and Miller when their production of *Spider-Man: Into the Spider-Verse* opened to great critical acclaim and great box office sales. Sony and Marvel had approached the pair in 2014 to craft this first animated feature in the Spider-Man franchise. On the one hand, Miller and Lord were clearly sought for the differences that animation could bring to the franchise, which had already gone through a series of reboots in the live-action realm and that, as such, stayed within one narrative universe rather than going in new directions. On the other hand, Spider-Man *comics* had long been open to alternate-universe stories and complicated variations on the original narrative premise. *Spider-Man: Into the Spider-Verse* is a very rich multiple-universe story that takes animation's capacity for world-making to new narrative *and* visual heights. As one commentator on the film has summed it up, "It's really inventive in like a dozen different ways."

That judgment comes, in fact, from Chris Miller himself, from the commentary track for the *Spider-Man: Into the Spider-Verse* DVD. It's important, I think, to see this appreciation less as an act of bragging egotism than as one craftperson's estimation not so much of what he (and his partner) came up with on their own but as what so many who worked with them, and under them, were able to fashion. Miller and Lord oversaw the creative personnel for the film as executive producers (and Lord crafted the original story line and cowrote the script) with three others serving as directors, and it seems clearly to have been a rich collaboration. One of the directors, Rodney Rothman, pointedly describes on the DVD commentary track the great extent to which Lord and Miller explained their ideas for the film to the top members of the creative team but also invited everyone—and it really does seem to have potentially been *everyone* involved in the production—to offer creative suggestions. As codirector Peter Ramsey says, marveling at the animation for one sequence, "You end up applauding the team because it's so inspiring." The recurrent commentary-track laughter that I mentioned earlier is not just about guys having a good time during the recording session because they're with fun people (such as stars like Jonah Hill for the *Jump Street* commentaries, clearly a fun guy to pass some time with), but because they can turn themselves into spectators and appreciate just how good their own work can be. It's noteworthy that, along with long bouts of laughter, Lord-Miller commentary tracks also sport extended moments of silence where the filmmakers and their guests get so caught up in the movie that they forget to talk about it.

Spider-Man: Into the Spider-Verse is a visually stunning work that runs the gamut of animation styles, both to specify its origin in the Marvel comics (for example, it has quick flashes of drawn animation done to look like the half-tone method of printing that was used for comic books) and to find distinguishing looks for each parallel universe (for instance, anime; Disney or Warner Bros. with their animal figures; black-and-white hard-boiled noir). At the same time, the film offers not just sumptuous visual spectacle—or a diversity of spectacles, since it is a film that is ever-changing in look—but a heartfelt story about family, relationships, self-confidence, friendship, and so on. It's notable that the quiet moments of intimacy between characters awkwardly trying to reach out to each other are the ones the participants on the DVD commentary track (Lord and Miller as producers plus the three directors) often single out for special esteem. Yet it's also worth noting, in keeping with the deflation of sentiment that I've argued is also part of the Lord-Miller ventures, that the film mixes soft emotion with bursts of comedy, self-reflexivity, parody, and downright silliness. The pig version of Spider-Man (Peter Porker) seems especially to come from a flat, caricatural world that stands out by deliberately not fitting the rounded look of the film's primary universe. But it all seems to work together to create an experience of animation where we regard the formal achievement in its own right, never fully forgetting we are watching a movie, an often jokey and self-deconstructing one, and not a story of real characters with real emotions but nonetheless an effective and moving story of characters with meaningful emotions. A pig version of Spider-Man is fundamentally ridiculous, yet able to be totally moving. It's a nice in-joke that one of the bad guys dismisses Peter Porker as a worthy opponent by calling him a "mere cartoon," only to be answered, "You got a problem with cartoons?" and then pummeled into submission by the pig. The moment is a comment both on the ability of *Spider-Man: Into the Spider-Verse* to mix and match styles of animation in one rich work *and* to accept that even the unreality of animation can accommodate realities that don't fit the style. It reminds us of a time when animation lacked respect, in contrast to today, when it now readily proves its power.

Working in multiple capacities, from directing, writing, producing, and downright shepherding of creative teams across multiple moving-image media, from television commercials to TV series and feature films, Chris Miller and Phil Lord have crafted animated works that stand out as objects of mass veneration. (And as we've seen, their record in live-action is no less essential.) The much-revered cult classic *Clone High* showed an older animation style updated to showcase modern, sometimes daring, subject matter; *Cloudy with a Chance of Meatballs*, in a somewhat similar revisionary style, reworked a children's classic for contemporary times as a tale of nerd redemption; and *Spider-Man: Into the Spider-Verse* ranged across a history of animation styles and created a dazzling filmic experience that is important for its ability to make quiet moments of sentiment meaningful within all the visual fun and games (including mind games). And *The LEGO Movie* revised stop-motion animation for the digital age while showing how ironic deflation can be a successful strategy for commercial filmmaking that reaches out to mass audiences of all ages and all levels of critical awareness.

Reception and After-Life

The LEGO Movie was a gigantic hit in 2014 (box office revenues were an estimated $469 million, one of the highest figures for that year). Critics generally loved it and singled it out for its retro look, which many said was a relief from the general sameness of the visuals in digital animation. The critics also praised the film's comic inventiveness, with special commendation for its irony about the very corporate salesmanship it could itself have been expected to engage in as a film rich in commodity tie-in potential. Weirdly, though, as he thought about getting into the movie business himself, libertarian conservative commentator Glenn Beck took inspiration from *The LEGO Movie* as a model of entertainment that he contended *avoided irony* and eschewed what he termed "the double meanings and adult humor that I just hate." Conversely, some other conservative politicians clearly missed what Beck saw as *The LEGO Movie*'s post-ironic, all-American innocence and debated whether the film was dangerously anticapitalist.[1]

Predictably, for a franchise film based on a toy, there was an array of commodity tie-ins: for example, seventeen building sets, sixteen special character minifigs, a video game, McDonalds Happy Meal items, books, apparel, school supplies, and on and on. After the release of the sequel, *The LEGO Movie 2*, scenes from both films were called upon as inspiration for attractions in a new section of LEGOLAND theme parks

called "The LEGO Movie World": here, one could take a sim-
ulated ride on Emmet's double-decker couch, visit his apartment for photo ops, or plunge toward the ground on a drop
ride in which the Unikitty's face (at the top of the structure)
would change along with, presumably, those of the participants as they were propelled toward Earth.

In the five-year period between the release of *The LEGO
Movie* and its sequel, which was much less successful finan-
cially and critically, two follow-up LEGO feature films appeared: *The LEGO Ninjago Movie* and *The LEGO Batman
Movie*. Strikingly, both move in narrative directions outside
the premise of *The LEGO Movie*. Specifically, neither of these
follow-up films works to any great degree with the idea
that their LEGO fictional world is actually the fictional creation of real-life human beings. Neither film, then, adheres
to the compelling visual conceit of the first film, wherein not
merely the minifigs and their built environments are made
of LEGO but the natural world as well. Watery places, for
instance, look pretty cool in both films, but they pointedly
are not constructed from LEGO pieces. Vaguely, *The LEGO
Ninjago Movie* hints at a sort of fictionalization as its LEGO
narrative is supposed to be a tale introduced (by Jackie Chan)
in a live-action prologue, yet which then pretty much drops out
as a frame once the LEGO story gets going (but for the weird
intrusion of a live-action cat, along with some other real-world
items, into the LEGO story—something that makes no sense
since the framed fictional tale is supposed to be an inviolate
narrative unto itself). Conversely, *The LEGO Batman* movie
entirely discards any human frame whatsoever and pretends
to be a fully enclosed fiction (although it does have one quick
shot borrowed from *The LEGO Movie*). In its stand-alone

status from the franchise, *The LEGO Batman Movie* is in fact quite beloved by many viewers, and I've even had some of its admirers tell me they think it's flat out the best Batman movie ever, animated *or live*.

In addition to these features that moved away from the narrative conceit of *The LEGO Movie* (only the presence of Batman connects back to the earlier film), the lead-up period to *The LEGO Movie 2* saw the production of short films that spun off directly from the original, using characters from it as if to both keep the franchise in the public eye (or in the eye specifically of the LEGO fan) and build up interest in the sequel. For instance, for the devoted LEGO fan, in 2016 The LEGO Group premiered a short film, *The LEGO Movie 4D* (in some listings, it's called *The LEGO MOVIE 4D Experience*, or sometimes *The LEGO Movie 4D: A New Adventure*), that showed at its theme parks and its indoor Discovery Centers. This spin-off short film both amplifies the idea of cinematic experience as a top-down, guided procedure that audiences become caught up in *and* seeks possibilities for active audience participation, however controlled and directed. The 4D of the title refers to an exhibition process that typically combines the wearing of 3D glasses with vibrating seats and other techniques to supposedly break down the barrier between screen fiction and audience presence, such as sprays of water, wafts of smoke, confetti, and so on. (If you watch the flat versions of the film that are available on the web, you can easily tell where these effects in the auditorium would appear.) Predictably, as a short film shown in amusement parks, both outdoor and indoor, where one steps out from the theater to confront a range of inviting physical rides and participatory games that continue the somewhat immersive experience of the film,

The LEGO Movie 4D takes on theme park qualities in both style and narrative. (Unlike the feature films, in fact, which one could choose to see at local movie theaters or purchase or rent later in DVD or streaming formats, the 4D film obviously requires the decision to have entered deeply into LEGO culture by electing to go to its amusement parks.) On the one hand, like a park attraction, the short is visually all about things rushing toward the spectator or the spectator being rushed by camera movement toward the background; on the other hand, its narrative is about Emmet and his minifig buddies being invited by Lord Business's brother Risky (get it?) to Brick World, an ersatz rival of LEGOLAND, and discovering that his plan is to force them into a stage show to exploit their LEGO celebrity from the original feature film and thereby bring customers to the knock-off amusement park. Emmet and Wyldstyle resist Risky's attempts at mind control and build a LEGO gizmo to thwart him. Here, for aid in finding the requisite parts, they directly address the audience, asking us to help spot the needed components and shout out when we see these floating in the space around them. Risky is defeated, and Emmet and Wyldstyle thank the audience for their help before bounding off the screen as if they are joining with the audience in the LEGO theme park experience. Between the original film and its 2018 sequel, *The LEGO Movie 4D* is both about keeping the franchise in the public eye (or at least that captive public that has willingly paid to continue its LEGO experience by going to the theme park) and insisting on the irreducible experience that LEGO offers compared to inadequate copycats (a quickly viewed billboard for Brick World prevaricates "Not a fake park designed to trap you!"). The film stands as an advertisement for the feature film franchise, but it also promotes the integrity of the LEGO brand itself: when pirate Metal Beard, under mind control, sings "Everything Is Super," Brick World's rip-off of "Everything Is Awesome," he notes that his version is "legal under fair use," a canny comment by The LEGO Group on all the brick-toy companies that poach, improperly as TLG sees it, LEGO products (despite the irony of the LEGO brick itself originally taking inspiration from a British company's invention). *The LEGO Movie 4D* was coproduced by TLG and the consumer products branch of Warner Bros., with a Van Nuys effects company, Pure Imagination, taking on the digital animation responsibilities (and maintaining the look of the original *LEGO Movie* wherein everything, character and environment, seems to be made up of LEGO pieces). Interestingly, the film was directed by Rob Schrab, who was then slated to helm *The LEGO Movie 2* as his first *feature* film until "creative differences" led to him being replaced by *Trolls* director Mike Mitchell.

The most curious of spin-offs, made as the sequel was being readied for release, came in 2018 when Warner Bros. paired with Turkish Airlines to produce a set of *LEGO Movie*-inspired safety videos for the aviation company. (Warner already had worked with Turkish Air on a promotional campaign inspired by the 2016 film *Batman vs. Superman: Dawn of Justice*). The films were made as part of a larger branding operation that also included planes sporting LEGO banners and in-flight video tied to *The LEGO Movie 2*. In the unintentionally amusing words of İlker Aycı, Turkish Airlines chairman of the board, "We are both brands that are enjoyed around the world, bringing together generations and cultures everywhere."[2]

Advertised as containing "the smallest cast ever assembled," the two safety videos (evidently with variant versions to correspond to different aircraft in the Turkish fleet) have some of the self-reflexive qualities of *The LEGO Movie* and the (at that point) upcoming sequel.[3] In the first, Emmet and Wyldstyle introduce themselves pointedly as celebrities because of the success of the first feature, but also note they are between films and are doing what stars do in such a case namely, making safety videos! The video goes through typical instructions, but with everything (for example, the carry-on you need to stow under the seat in front of you, as well as that seat itself) in LEGO. Quite astutely, the instruction card that travelers can consult from their seat pocket is presented in LEGO style—simple visuals with no verbiage. Batman makes a self-announced "cameo" appearance to continue the recitation of safety procedures (and there are additional cameos by other characters from *The LEGO Batman* movie as well as *The LEGO Ninjago Movie*). Bridging both *The LEGO Movie* and *The LEGO Movie 2*, Unikitty tries to sing a catchy pop safety song ("It's a party in the sky; let's pack our dreams and fly") that she says is intended to get stuck inside passengers' heads. The video ends with what are declared by Emmet to be "overly earnest closing remarks" on safety. In the follow-up video, a studio executive (with the poster for "Another Cinematic Universe" on her wall, a crafty admission that Warner Bros. has to promote franchises other than the hugely successful one that Marvel has been luxuriating in) declares that, as a producer, her basic role is to generate sequels, and so the gang must now make a new safety video, this one directed by Batman dressed in an artsy auteur look (including a beret). Unlike the first safety film, which stayed within one plane readying for take-off, the follow-up is more expansive, like a big Hollywood production, as we move from city to city (presumably ones that

Turkish Airlines services) throughout the world while each part of the instructions is demonstrated on cutaway movie sets. For example, in Tokyo, Unikitty—growing ever redder with anger as she is wont to do in the feature films—confronts kids on their phones at a neon-filled street crossing to remind them that on planes, at least, electronic devices must be switched off or placed in flight mode. The very locale cleverly picks up on the ways public places in Tokyo, like Shinjuku or Shibuya, are all about cellphone culture. In a fascinating echo of the first feature film, this safety video ends with a jump from a LEGO world to a live-action human one shown to exist on a larger scale (in this case, unlike the basement world of *The LEGO Movie* itself, the human space here is the lounge of the Istanbul airport, where Turkish Airlines crew members pass by the minfigs' animated LEGO safety demonstration).

The LEGO Movie 2: The Second Part was released on February 9, 2019. As noted, the success of the first film had enabled Animal Logic to open new production facilities in Vancouver, much closer to Los Angeles than Sydney and perhaps benefiting from newly competitive government concessions to outsource to this growing production hub in Canada. In the Vancouver move we can see confirmation that digital production is often not really about geography per se but rather the advantages around funding (and taxation and rebate) and cultivation of production venues that, in large part because they are not directly part of the Hollywood system (and not usually subsidiaries of larger firms), must keep experimenting and showing off new advances in technique and technology: in a way, they serve as an R&D complement to Hollywood production, which reaps the creative benefits while avoiding many of the risks. Even more than the first *LEGO Movie*, where characters can move from one part of the LEGO universe to another (many are presumed to be adjacent, separated only by walls that can be brought down at film's end), *The LEGO Movie 2* offers an expansive fantasy geography that fully brackets off the real geography of film production for outer-space journeys to made-up worlds way out in the expansive universe. (*Spider-Man: Into the Spider-Verse* was also animated in Vancouver, but in-house at Sony's own animation division, Sony Pictures Imageworks.)

The sequel is filled with the recognition that it is part of a franchise: in this, it looks back to the free-floating wackiness of the *Jump Street* films, which endlessly comment on originality and derivative culture (of course, they have the advantage over the first *The LEGO Movie* of building off of, and spoofing, a prior narrative, the *21 Jump Street* television series). *The LEGO Movie 2* constantly notes when it is relying on tropes that have become common and conventionalized (for example, when the heroes have to escape through a large, closing gate, they comment on the dramatic and suspense-building slowness of the portal's motion; at another moment, one of the LEGO refer to a clever gadget as a "CPD—convenient plot device"), and it moves beyond a self-reflexivity about narrative and stylistic motifs to make jokes about the movie business itself and the telling role of franchises within it (for example, Batman claims that he should be designated leader of the team because he's had about nine films devoted to him with three more "in development").

The LEGO Movie 2 opens with the blend of live-action and animated shots that concluded the first part: in the human world, Finn's dad says that now that the boy is going to be allowed to engage in creative play with the LEGO, in fairness his sister has to be permitted to play in the basement too; within the LEGO world itself, we see DUPLO arriving and making demands. A title card announces "Five Years Later" (notably, also the time between the first film and the sequel), and we discover that the awesome world of Bricksburg has become Apocalypseburg, a wasteland combination of Planet of the Apes and Road Warrior (each, it should be noted, a film within a franchise). Ever optimistic, Emmet asks, "Can we rebuild the future?"—a question that, in the case of a franchised series, is not only a narrative one (within the fiction, can a happy life be achieved again?), but also one about the franchise business itself: that is, to ask here what the transformation of narrative givens entails and how far it can go is to also ask what each new installment in the franchise does to its predecessors, and what logic of sameness and difference it sets up. Canny about the frequently very crass commercialism of sequels, *22 Jump Street* kept commenting on its own close adherence to the plot of its predecessor. A remake of a reboot, it was deliberately caught up in a repetition that it not merely accepted but reveled in (which is not at all to say that the film doesn't find ways to be inventive that make it stand on its own). Conversely, while both LEGO movies derive from preexisting intellectual property—namely, the LEGO brick—they are not bound to a prior *narrative* premise and instead invent their story from scratch. In extending its predecessor into new fictional realms, *The LEGO Movie 2* in its own way references the very expansiveness inherent in the commerce behind LEGO: just as TLG sought out new revenue streams by introducing DUPLO, so does the introduction of DUPLO into the space of LEGO in the film sequel seem to change fundamental conditions, shake things up, and revise all the givens of the first movie—literally so, in that when we first see Emmet rise to begin his blindly cheerful daily saunter through post-apocalypse Bricksburg, we are reintroduced to many characters that Emmet encountered in his gambol through town in the first film, but they now have become toughened, turned Goth by new conditions (for example, surfer dude Dave has now become "chainsaw Dave").

A Cool Dude gets weaponized

Even before the release of *The LEGO Movie 2*, there was speculation about whether or not the franchise would continue. Strikingly, one article raised this very question *the day before the sequel's opening* and quoted Will Arnett (the voice, of course, of LEGO Batman) on the central role Lord and Miller would have in determining new installments: "Of course ultimately that's up to Phil Lord and Chris Miller. Because they are truly the gate-keepers of the franchise."[4] Intriguingly, the piece hinted (as did some other articles here and there in the industry press) at development of a new installment as well in the LEGO Batman spin-off franchise and in a LEGO race car movie "in the mold of *Cannonball Run*" (some reports specify the title as *The Billion Brick Race*, and it's had a fraught development with a series of directors hired and fired).[5]

But *The LEGO Movie 2* did not have the desired box office performance, always worrisome for a franchise. In its first week, it did no more than half the business of its predecessor (and, as noted, the two intervening films in the franchise, *The LEGO Batman Movie* and *The LEGO Ninjago Movie*, had also underperformed—although not to the degree of *The LEGO Movie 2*).[6] It may be revealing that at the very moment journalists were trying to explain the relative box-office failure of *The LEGO Movie 2: The Second Part*, speaking already of the exhaustion of a franchise that had started out so great, the *New York Times* reported that Warner Bros. had signed with Japanese firm Sanrio to make a Hello Kitty movie (whether or not as animation was not yet known), hinting more than a little directly that Warner was thereby searching, perhaps, for a new toy tie-in for franchise possibilities beyond LEGO.[7]

In any case, major announcements in the trade press, one just three months after the release of *The LEGO Movie 2*, of new directions for the Lord Miller company made it seem unlikely that the team would give priority to LEGO (if continuing with the franchise at all). First, it was announced that the pair had contracted with Sony (for whom they had produced the hit film *Spider-Man: Into the Spider-Verse*) for a big multi-project television deal of both animation and live-action. The new Sony deal centered on the promise of a Spider-Man series, since he was a Marvel character that Sony owned rights to. It also allowed the duo to develop outside projects for platforms like cable, network television, and streaming. There is, for instance, from an earlier contract with FOX, a television series they executive-produced, *Bless the Harts*, which premiered in fall 2019 and was renewed for a second season, and a feature film, *Artemis* (about a lunar female smuggler who runs up against organized crime trying to take over a moon installation named Artemis), not yet in production. At Sony, the new deal was specifically with the television division, but Lord and Miller continued to work with the company, such as on the development of a feature film, *The Last Human*, from a children's story about a robot who bonds with one of the last human survivors of a worldwide apocalypse in a quest to find a magical place of hope.[8]

And then, in a second and really potentially grand action, it was announced in August 2019 that the Lord Miller company had signed a very big multipicture feature film deal with Universal. The trade press presented the arrangement as a logical step after the TV deal with Sony, although there was little detail, at this early stage, about specific projects Lord and Miller might undertake at Universal.[9]

Whatever the case, LEGO follow-ups did not seem part of the mix.

Coda

Maybe, in fact, for all the attempted franchise building—the sequel, related feature films (Batman, Ninjago), spin-offs, product tie-ins, and convergence with other forms of spectacle (from games to theme park attractions)—*The LEGO Movie* is best thought of as a divergent cultural work unto itself. It anticipates and even delights in the various challenges and limitations of establishing a film franchise—maybe even going so far as to position itself as a kind of anti-franchise film, one that on some level resists franchising even while participating in it. Certainly, for instance, the sequel could have maintained the narrative premise of a fictional world that discovers it is nestled inside a real-life one, but this later film would have had to do so without the impact of the first movie's big reveal, so seemingly central to its appeal to spectators.

Through irony, and through projecting savvy self-awareness and knowingness about the ins and outs of the culture industry while still delivering the goods of dynamic diversion, *The LEGO Movie* stands apart while also assuming pride of place in popular culture today. Even as it toys and plays with storytelling, establishing key plot points only to make fun of them (when it doesn't simply lose them in the spectacular rush of images), there's maybe a larger story here in the very existence of this constantly shifting and dismantling piece of popular culture: perhaps an irony of this sort that refuses to settle

171

down has become in fact a much preferred stance vis-à-vis contemporary digital-industrial arts for a new creative class involved in the crafting of mass entertainment today. The film demonstrates that an anonymous minifig from the static, physical world of LEGO can be animated dynamically for resonant cinematic effect as well as resonant (and often moving) storytelling. In its silliness and its seriousness together, *The LEGO Movie* is downright dumpressive. This is why it is essential cinema.

Acknowledgments

I always find it somewhat curious when, in their acknowl-
edgements, academics seem more than a bit surprised at the
gracious help they received from friends and colleagues. In
my experience, the scholarly world endlessly confirms its generous dedication to the collective enterprise of knowledge-
building. So, deepest gratitude (without even attempting to
catch the many who gave a passing reference here and there) to:
Patrick Keating (for introducing me to 21st Century Film Essentials, discussing potential ideas, and ultimately offering great
feedback on a draft of the completed manuscript); Donna
Kornhaber, series editor, who welcomed the proposal enthusiastically (along with Jim Burr and Sarah McGavick at the
University of Texas Press itself); the two anonymous readers,
recruited by the Press, who offered intensely valuable advice
for strengthening the study; dear friends Scott Bukatman,
the late Thomas Elsaesser, Jon Lewis, Fred Wasser, David
Cook, Andrew Ross, and Blair Davis, always there with great
and productive insights; new email acquaintances Kara Lynn
Andersen, Derek Johnson, and Shawna Kidman, who con-
versed about their own work on media industry; old pal and
animation theorist par excellence Don Crafton; Toby Miller,
Adrian Danks, Ben Goldsmith, Alex Burns, Ben Eltham, and
Noel King, who provided context for animation work outsourced to Australia; good buddy Tom Kemper, who knows

contemporary animation and LEGO so well (and commented so richly on a draft); Petra Domínková, John Canemaker, Genevieve Yu, Stephen Groening, Aaron Rich, William Brown, Leah Aldridge, and colleague Dan Streible for leads on toys that became films; current and former doctoral students (now professors) Jinying Li, Dan Herbert, Panpan Yang, and Rochelle Miller for bibliographic hints; media and legal scholars Dan Hunter and Julian Thomas for useful exchange about LEGO as intellectual property (with additional thanks to Peter Decherney for putting me in touch); and the Dartmouth film studies gang—Amy Lawrence, Mark Williams, David Ehrlich—for reminiscences about directors Phil Lord and Chris Miller (with a special shout-out to David for facilitating contact with the ever-lively pair).

I also found a gracious welcome from creative figures who exhibit justifiable satisfaction in their work on *The LEGO Movie*: Phil Lord and Chris Miller themselves (along with their incredibly helpful assistant Rachel Smith) greeted the project with a refreshing blend of bemusement and pride, and fielded questions in an energetic and often hilarious phone conversation (with rich email follow-up); producer Dan Lin (and his supportive chief of staff Tiffany Nakano) warmly fielded many questions about the film's development; and Greg Talmadge at Blur helped me understand that company's preproduction efforts on the film. The LEGO Group's policy is to not assist in scholarly research not licensed with them; they request the following be appended to any such scholarship: "All information is collected and interpreted by its authors and does not represent the opinion of the LEGO Group."

My dear friend JoAnn Hanley assisted greatly in background research. At Megabrain comics store (Rhinebeck, NY), the sage

Jean Michel along with the awesome Simon Dantzic helped clarify cartoon and comics history. Genevieve Havemeyer-King did the photos and frame-grabs. My sister-in-law Barbara Peterson provided useful insights on a key issue. And my immediate family, Marita Sturken and Leo Polan, have always been there for me with love, support, and insight. Leo, who turned thirteen as I finished this book, has taught me much about today's popular culture and its many dimensions: it's to him that this book is dedicated.

Notes

PROLOGUE

1. Fred Hauptfuhrer, "Rock's Space Oddity, David Bowie, Falls to Earth and Lands on His Feet in Film," *People*, September 6, 1976, people.com/archive/cover-story-rocks-space-oddity-vol-6-no-10.
2. Email from Dan Lin via his staff, July 18, 2019.
3. Benjamin Svetkey, "Making of 'LEGO Movie': 7 Years, a Trip to Denmark and a Race against the Disney-Lucasfilm Deal Clock," *Hollywood Reporter*, January 23, 2015, hollywoodreporter.com/news/making-lego-movie-7-years-762327. Lin's concern to bring creativity into franchise filmmaking is chronicled in Ben Fritz, *The Big Picture: The Fight for the Future of Movies* (New York: Houghton Mifflin Harcourt, 2018), 168–174, 184–186.
4. It's worth noting as well that both Emmet and Rex are voiced by well-known star Chris Pratt. The character of Rex in *The LEGO Movie 2: The Second Part* riffs on Pratt's celebrity: for instance, the velociraptors who form his spaceship crew stand as a clear allusion to Pratt's character in *Jurassic World*, who famously trains and tames such creatures for a living (and who also fights a genetically engineered dino named the Indominus Rex). In live-action franchises like the Jurassic features or Guardians of the Galaxy (as well as the larger context of Avengers) and television work like *Parks and Recreation*, Pratt's own image deliberately twists around on itself: it is both the assertion of male entitlement and its undoing insofar as it is goofy, overdone, and often coming up short.

THE WORLD OF ANIMATION AND
THE ANIMATION OF THE WORLD

1. Hyejin Noon and Edward J. Malecki, "Cartoon Planet:
   Worlds of Production and Global Production Networks in the
   Animation Industry," *Industrial and Corporate Change* 19, no.
   1 (2009): 247. Including features worldwide and direct-to-
   video offerings that did not have theatrical release, the figure
   is a bit skewed, but still telling.
2. Stanley Cavell, *The World Viewed: Reflections on the Ontology
   of Film*, enlarged ed. (Cambridge, MA: Harvard University
   Press, 1979), 168.
3. Lev Manovich, *The Language of New Media* (Cambridge, MA:
   MIT Press, 2001), 302.
4. In fact, several scenes in early script versions of *The LEGO
   Movie* appear to allude to *The Truman Show*: for example,
   Emmet discovering that his seemingly extended world actually
   is a walled-in construction, and a rebellious character trying to
   signal to him awareness of the fiction Emmet is living within.
   See, for one early version of the screenplay, screenplaydb.com/
   film/scripts/lego.pdf.
5. From the vast literature on animation's power as an art of
   morphing in an age fascinated by the instabilities, positive
   and negative, of identity, a book I've found particularly useful
   for thinking about a movie about LEGO—the hard piece that,
   when linked to other hard pieces, enables transformative creation—is *Girlhood and the Plastic Image* by Heather Warren-
   Crow, whose very mention of "Plastic" in its title links to the
   animation world that *The LEGO Movie* offers. Citing, like others, Manovich on animation as the defining condition of cinema, Warren-Crow sees it through the metaphor of "plasticity"
   as morphable, pliable, endlessly reinventable. This is indeed a
   converse sense of "plastic" to one that emphasizes its fixities,
   its solidity, its durability. It's in this sense the plastic as "plas-
   matic," to use famed filmmaker/theorist Sergei Eisenstein's
   term for animation as, as he saw it, a mode of endless transformation. See Heather Warren-Crow, *Girlhood and*

the Plastic Image (Lebanon, NH: University Press of New England, 2014); and Sergei Eisenstein, *Eisenstein on Disney*, ed. Jay Leyda, trans. Alan Upchurch (New York: Seagull Books, 1986). And of course one should also consult the great masterworks on animation as transformation and a "giving of life to things": Don Crafton, *Shadow of a Mouse: Performance, Belief, and World-Making in Animation* (Berkeley: University of California Press, 2014); Scott Bukatman, *The Poetics of Slumberland: Animated Spirits and the Animating Spirit* (Berkeley: University of California Press, 2012); and Vivian Sobchack's anthology, *Meta-Morphing: Visual Transformation and the Culture of Quick-Change* (Minneapolis: University of Minnesota Press, 2000), especially Sobchack's own contribution, "'At the Still Point of the Turning World': Meta-Morphing and Meta-Stasis," 131–158.

6. Thomas Elsaesser, *The Mind-Game Film: Distributed Agency, Time Travel and Productive Pathology* (New York: Routledge, forthcoming).

7. Shawna Kidman, *Comic Books Incorporated: How the Business of Comics Became the Business of Hollywood* (Berkeley: University of California Press, 2019), 7.

8. Yet it should be noted that there sometimes can be local impediments to the global spread of animation. *The LEGO Movie* did not get released in China, for instance, a potential big market for American films but one that works with a quota on the number of US films that can enter in any one year. In an email to me (October 21, 2019), Phil Lord wonders if the fact of an "anti-totalitarian film for children" might not have caused the Chinese government to desist in the film's distribution there.

9. Derek Johnson, *Transgenerational Media Industries: Adults, Children, and the Reproduction of Culture* (Ann Arbor: University of Michigan Press, 2019). We might contrast LEGO's enduring appeal, across decades and generations, as a potential factor in the success of *The LEGO Movie*, with the failure of the 2019 animation feature *UglyDolls*. Many factors appear to have worked against that film, including a cheapening of the budget

when successful animation often seems to go for big-bucks expenditures. But limits in durational cross-generational appeal also seem to have been at play: the UglyDolls are less than two decades old and don't have a firm and long-honed base of reverence. Strikingly, when I mentioned the film to friends, it was not only those without young children who overwhelmingly hadn't heard of the brand; even those who did have children simply had never encountered this line of toys.

10. See, most famously, Noël Carroll, "The Future of an Allusion: Hollywood in the Seventies (and Beyond)," *October* 102 (Spring 1982): 52–81.

11. And vice versa, of course. It is tempting, for instance, to imagine that the youngest viewers would take *The LEGO Movie* less ironically than adults would, but, amusingly, A. O. Scott in his *New York Times* review of the film entertains the opposite possibility: adults feeling sentimental when the father and son hug in the non-LEGO "real world" and the kids cringing at a cheesiness whose manipulations they can see through. See Scott, "Toying with Ideas Outside the Manual," *New York Times*, February 6, 2014.

THE LEGO MOVIE AS SAVVY CINEMA

1. See the aptly titled *Seven Minutes: The Life and Death of the American Animated Cartoon* (rev. ed.) by Norman Klein (New York: Verso, 1993).

2. See David C. Robertson (with Bill Breen), *Brick by Brick: How LEGO Rewrote the Rules of Innovation and Conquered the Global Toy Industry* (New York: Crown Business, 2013), 140, 269.

3. I've put "camera" in quotation marks since, as a digital film, the animation in *The LEGO Movie* was made in the computer. (A very few shots, though, were actually filmed photographically.) From this point on, I will drop the quotation marks for the sake of readability.

4. Of course, there had long been plastic model kits with large custom pieces that enforced guided construction (for example,

the fuselages for such things as fighter planes in the 1950s). In this respect, perhaps, there is nothing "new" to LEGO customized pieces—except that they can appear to run counter to the LEGO spirit of open play.

5. The frequent jittery look of photographic animation also comes from the fact that its images are often animated "on the twos" (or threes and so on), as animators term it. This means using a frame more than once (as opposed to the use of single frames, as would be the case for each instant in 24-frames-per-second live-action), whether to save money (as was notoriously true of television animation in the 1960s and after) or to vary pacing (one can change the speed of a scene by going up or down in the number of repeated frames).

Not everyone is enamored of the employment in *The LEGO Movie* of digital means to emulate an older craft form. As one friend declared upon reading a draft of the manuscript for this book, "When I saw *The LEGO Movie*, I assumed (wrongly) that the film was mostly stop-motion with lots of computerized touches . . . but the thing is, I must say that I like the movie a little bit less now that I know it was all done on a computer, and not via stop-motion with hand-built LEGO settings. Why is that? Surely, the technical achievement of making a movie on a computer that looks like stop-motion is just as impressive (if not more so) than making a movie with a bunch of LEGO builders making all these settings and figures. And yet I feel somehow that the filmmakers betrayed the LEGO ideal by not shooting stop-motion—by not actually building these things and then taking them apart and putting them back together again. Somehow, I think that a film that was a photographic record of all that work would have been better (truer to the LEGO spirit) than the movie we have—even if it would have looked totally identical."

6. For what it's worth, we see a "Rent" sign on Emmet's apartment building—which implies a financial transaction. And in the live-action coda, Finn mentions the toy store from which the LEGO that his dad has filled the basement with have been purchased.

7. Steven Zeitchik, "Many Moving Parts Snap into Place in 'The LEGO Movie,'" *Los Angeles Times*, January 19, 2014.

8. See Dan Hunter and Julian Thomas, "LEGO and the System of Intellectual Property, 1955–2015," *Intellectual Property Quarterly* 1 (2016): 10.

9. Phil Lord, Chris Miller, and Jason Latour, "A Secret Roar Rages?" *Peter Porker: The Spectacular Spider-Ham*, Spider-Man Annual, no. 1 (August 2019).

10. In an email to me (August 21, 2019), Phil Lord notes that the production team had extensive discussions for the sequel of what he nicely terms the "Trinity Syndrome."

THROUGH THE RABBIT HOLE, INTO THE LEGO-VERSE

1. In an email to me (August 19, 2019), Phil Lord speaks of a "Fun fact—at one point the movie moved *too* fast. It actually takes a little longer to process the images. You not only have to process the cinematic imagery like you would on every movie, but you also have to decode the LEGO bricks and what they signify. That extra split second could be felt in early screenings where it was hard to keep up with the movie. . . . That meant that some people reported the movie feeling long, but we suspected what they really experienced was a lack of engagement. The studio asked us to take five minutes out of the picture, but instead we put five minutes IN, extra time to watch the characters process what was happening and make decisions before they acted—describing their interiority—and it worked. The movie *felt* shorter but it was in fact longer."

   For a fascinating discussion of a key case of animation caught between dynamism and immobility, see Marc Steinberg's rich *Anime's Media Mix: Franchising Toys and Characters in Japan* (Minneapolis: University of Minnesota Press, 2012).

2. Andrew Essex, *The End of Advertising: Why It Had to Die, and the Creative Resurrection to Come* (New York: Spiegel & Grau, 2017), 173.

3. Majken Schultz and Mary Jo Hatch, "The Cycles of Corporate Branding: The Case of the LEGO Company," *California Management Review* 46, no. 1 (2003): 8.

4. Jack Stone was a fictional adventurer (somewhat modeled on Indiana Jones, who himself inspired LEGO sets) created by The LEGO Group itself to provide in-house character-based intellectual property. But unlike known heroes from movies and television that TLG licensed with film studios and other media companies, Jack Stone came with no prior reputation or consumer recognition, didn't do well, and was discontinued.

5. Schultz and Hatch, "The Cycles of Corporate Branding," 13.

6. Ibid.

7. To clarify, the live-action material for the ending actually was shot in standard 2D and converted to 3D.

8. It is indeed intriguing, in light of *The LEGO Movie*'s depiction of Good Cop/Bad Cop as a variable figure whose two-face can shift back and forth (and one of which literally gets erased at one point) to note that some of the earliest, far-from-perfect figurines, before the elaboration of the minifig in 1978, were of *faceless* policemen; moreover, policemen (and later policewomen) would stand as some of the most recurrent figurines across LEGO's history, including after the emergence of the minifig, thus giving allegorical substance to *The LEGO Movie*'s depiction of Good Cop/Bad Cop as a character who keeps popping up, who seems to constantly rebound from each setback to continue, inexorably, his chase after the good guys.

9. On the commentary track for the *LEGO Movie* DVD, the participants (the film's directors plus key actors) note, during one big chase, that one can improvise with random LEGO pieces to craft vehicles similar to the ones we're viewing, but they then sardonically, laughingly admit they should be helping out LEGO by advising the listener to buy sets, not assorted pieces!

FALLING INTO NARRATIVE

1. In his August 21, 2019, email to me, Phil Lord reiterates that he and cowriter/director Chris Miller played with the

convention earlier with their TV show *Clone High* (about which more later). One character, Joan of Arc, lives with a blind African American foster granddad who is wont to say, "I may be blind but . . .," but then gets wrong what he is going to say and even gets wrong what situation he is in.

Lord clarifies that the character of Vitruvius wasn't written with a specific ethnicity in mind, but that Morgan Freeman got top choice for a voice that "everyone trusts." Interestingly, and amusingly, as Lord recounts, TLG wants all minifigs to be yellow in color—unless they derive from preexisting intellectual property such as *Star Wars* (for example, the character Mace Windu, played by a black man)—so he and Miller filmed an episode of a fake television show, *Wonder Wizards*, to legitimize the black Vitruvius voiced by Morgan Freeman.

2. Svetkey, "Making of 'LEGO Movie.'"
3. One of the anonymous reviewers of the draft manuscript for this book suggests that *Where Are My Pants?* may invoke the 2006 dystopian film *Idiocracy*, in which a TV show called *Ow, My Balls* is shown to dumb down an already dumbed, and benumbed, population.
4. Nicki Gostin, "Devo Lead Singer Dishes on Creating Catchy 'LEGO' Song," Fox News, February 18, 2014, foxnews.com/entertainment/devo-lead-singer-dishes-on-creating-catchy-lego-song.
5. In passing, it is worth noting that this song, performed initially in the film as a tool of political-economic control, was turned against dominant power in a famous case of activist hijacking. LEGO had been partnering with Shell Oil, and Greenpeace put pressure on the toy company for this worrisome alliance by commissioning a video that used a mournful version of "Everything Is Awesome" over images of LEGO characters in the Arctic (from cute animals like polar bears or huskies or seagulls to fishermen to children to Santa himself and his elves). The characters are engulfed by a viscous spread of oil while a LEGO fat capitalist (cigar in mouth) supervises this terrible wounding of the environment.

Warner Bros. evidently threatened copyright infringement, but ultimately backed away from a controversy that risked making it seem an environmental bad guy. TLG held out a little longer, saying Greenpeace's dispute with Shell was a regional matter that a global toy company should not get involved in. But as the video went viral (with attacks on it in the conservative financial press evidently only adding to the visibility of the campaign), TLG relented and dissolved its alliance with Shell. Media scholar Toby Miller offers a trenchant account of this incident in *Greenwashing Culture* (New York: Routledge, 2018), 92–95. For the video itself, go to youtube.com/watch?v=qhbliUq0_r4.

THE EXTRAORDINARY ORDINARINESS OF LEGO

1. Somewhat in contrast, the short film *Padawan Menace*, a LEGO reworking of the first released *Star Wars* film, *A New Hope*, and made by the same animation team as *The LEGO Movie* (as discussed later), offers a clever, in-joke riff on the role of instructions for purposeful LEGO building: stranded with Yoda in the desert, android C-3PO asserts that they need to build a spaceship to get away, but when he finds a typical LEGO instruction sheet—all images, no words, as is the case famously for real-world LEGO instructions—he, ever so verbal, declares despairingly that he can't figure the pictures out. It's up to Yoda to eschew instructions and use the Force to bring bricks and components together to form magically into a space vessel.

2. In an essay on LEGO Tolkien sets, "Middle Earth and LEGO Recreation," in the collective volume *LEGO Studies*, Neal Baker notes how conflictual action can become an end unto itself, independent of narrative outcome. As Baker shows, the sets sometimes focus on battles given minimal attention (often only a few lines of narrative) by Tolkien. Sometimes, similarly, sets depict battle scenes that in the films take up just a few seconds or so. Narratively, this or that battle may not have mattered in novel *or* film, yet it can lead to a visually cool built model.

3. Early drafts of the script for *The LEGO Movie* show that the screenwriters had *Ocean's Eleven* clearly in mind. See, for instance, screenplaydb.com/film/scripts/lego.pdf, p. 76.

4. There is a small tradition in fantasy and science fiction of worlds that seemingly are other than ours but actually are extended from and derived from ours: the most obvious is the very first *Planet of the Apes* (with the Statue of Liberty found on the beach in the horrific twist at the film's ending), which is directly referenced in *The LEGO Movie 2*, but even closer in nature are cult films like *Zardoz* (1974) or *Glen and Randa* (1971), in which characters in some future place take inspiration from found relics from the past (our present, in fact) that they misread as talismans from former civilizations (the Wizard of Oz stories for the former film [misread as ZARD OZ]; a warped copy of a Rolling Stones album for the latter).

5. Ferrell's appearance in *The LEGO Movie* takes on an additional referential dimension if one remembers that he appeared in the 2006 film *Stranger than Fiction* as a character who discovers that he is, to a large degree, a fictional construct. Ferrell's character, Harold Crick, hears a voice narrating his life that turns out to belong to a novelist (played by Emily Thompson) who is crafting his story—which is expected to end in his early death. Like Emmet, say, Crick straddles the reality he has long inhabited—in which he presumed himself to be a real human being—and one that frames his reality and asserts it to be a fiction. In this case, though (and somewhat unlike in *The LEGO Movie*), Crick can reassert his own real-world existence (even to the point of meeting up with the novelist and showing to her that he is flesh and blood) and ultimately break free from being merely fictional.

THE SECRET LIFE OF TOYS

1. The 1998 film *Small Soldiers*, directed by Joe Dante, combines both the evil and benign traditions of toys that animate in the presence of humans. Here, researchers in the toy division of a mega-corporation, out for profits at all costs, engineer sentient battle toys, divided into the two groups of Commando Elite

(somewhat like G.I. Joe) and alien creatures known as Gorgonites, who go to war with each other. Deliberately upsetting the spectator's stereotyping expectations, the film has the Gorgonite aliens turn out to be good while the GIs are revealed as unbridled, vicious, evil aggressors (against humans as well as their nominal adversary). Both sides address the human protagonist, with the Gorgonite leader bonding with him and the GI commander shouting bellicose threats at him.

2. See, most famously, Miriam Hansen, *Babel and Babylon: Spectatorship in American Silent Film* (Cambridge, MA: Harvard University Press, 1991), 48–57.

3. There is at least one interesting violation of the seemingly common rule in *GI Joe* that the real world of toys be left behind for the fantasy fiction of soldiers, whether drawn or live-action, fully in their own world doing their own thing. In 2009, a two-part fifteen-minute TV offering, *GI Joe: The Invasion of Cobra Island*, used stop-motion to animate GI Joe figurines as a promotion for the fully *live-action* feature *GI Joe: The Rise of Cobra*. While fairly proficient special effects (for example, explosions and gun bursts, and above all lip animation when the figurines talk) help move the depiction beyond mere photographing of lifeless figurines, seemingly deliberate jerky stop-motion animation reiterates that these are toys, and that they are linked to the upcoming live-action film, but as tie-ins that predictably are purchasable to allow creative play at home.

4. Some films or TV works try to have it both ways, giving us animated beings, derived from a toy yet disavowing that origin within the fiction, while also reminding us of the originally fabricated, and therefore collectible, nature of the beings. For example, *Pokémon Detective Pikachu* (2019), a mix of live-action and animation, starts with a narrative prologue in which, outside the big city where humans and Pokémon live in harmony, humans *hunt* Pokémon (as in the original game). The film hints thereby at the collectibility of Pokémon beings even as it denies their toy status within the body of its narrative proper.

Hero Factory, a 2010 LEGO television series (later released on DVD), chronicles the outer-space adventures of androids within a fictional universe. Yet we learn from the opening voice-over that Hero Factory itself is a site where the androids are built on demand, with sockets and studs clicked together just like LEGO, when calls come in for their services as intergalactic law enforcers. In other words, the television series denies they are toys, but gives them a constructedness that can remind us of the LEGO that can be bought in the real world beyond the screen.

And in the cult independent film experiment *Superstar: The Karen Carpenter Story* (1987), directed by Todd Haynes, the sad story of Karen Carpenter is told *with Barbie dolls taking all the roles*. This fact is never alluded to, but it is of course visually obvious, and it works as commentary on norms of femininity that Karen Carpenter was pushed toward (and in her own tragic fashion tried to resist). The film brackets out any mention of the actual toy to weave its conceit that Carpenter herself was pushed by her society toward Barbie-like models of perfection and couldn't adapt to them.

5. As my friend Tom Kemper notes, the films of the Jurassic Park/World franchise provide an interesting complication: not themselves toys, of course, the dinosaurs are nonetheless treated within the story world as veritable playthings or spectacles for consumption by park goers. In the films, stores in the park's amusement center offer toy versions and related merchandise of the supposedly real dinosaurs on display (whether in the wild or caged up). The unleashing of the dinosaurs will then entail an attack on the very world of consumerism that has threatened to hem them in. Unlike, say, the Bratz or Transformers movies, the Jurassic films acknowledge commodification of their own collectibles, all the better to engage in (ironic) critique of the very merchandising that in large part drives the franchise.

6. One interesting variant of the prenarrative opening of a film or TV show as a veritable enumeration of the real toys one might buy occurs in the 2018 Dreamworks film *Trolls*. Before

the animated narrative action proper begins, we see a scrapbook of Troll cutouts and accessories while a female voice-over provides background. There's an allusion to ownership here (Trolls as something one might collect), but we soon learn that the voice and scrapbook belong to the Troll named Princess, whose story the film will then follow—not, that is, to a human being outside the fictional narrative. In other words, *Trolls* hints at toy possession only to move away from it into a fictional world of animate trolls.

Revealingly, in an interview with Ian Failes at the important animation site *Cartoonbrew*, *Trolls* director Mike Mitchell (later to direct *The LEGO Movie 2*) asserts that *The LEGO Movie* particularly helped him work out for *Trolls* the conventions for a toy-based film that didn't directly set out to sell toys. He specifically asked for advice from *The LEGO Movie* codirector Phil Lord since, as he puts it, Lord and Chris Miller "made a LEGO film that has nothing to do with any toy. You don't even consider that at all. You just go to the film and you enjoy it." Quoted in "'Trolls' Director Mike Mitchell: There Was No Mythology to These Things . . . I've Never Felt So Free," *Cartoon Brew*, December 4, 2016, cartoonbrew.com/ interviews/trolls-director-mike-mitchell-no-mythology -thingsive-never-felt-free-144212.html.

7. See, for instance, Amy Ratcliffe's extensive account "The LEGO Batman Movie: Yes, the Condiment King Is Real," on DC's own website, February 14, 2017. dccomics.com/ blog/2017/02/14the-lego-batman-movie-yes-the-condiment -king-is-real.

8. Arthur Melbourne Cooper's 1908 *Dreams of Toyland* does, from an early moment in cinema history, acknowledge monetary exchange in the acquisition of toys: the first part of this short film offers a boy and his mother buying toys in a store. The second half shows a dream of his in which the toys come to life, culminating, in an early example of the blurring of framed fictional world and framing real world, with an accident within the dream that causes the child to fall out of bed.

9. On *Toy Story*, see the excellent monographic study by Tom Kemper, *Toy Story* (London: BFI, 2015), and the recent scholarly anthology, *Toy Story: How Pixar Reinvented the Animated Feature*, edited by Susan Smith, Noel Brown, and Sam Summers (NY and London: Bloomsbury, 2018).

10. It is perhaps noteworthy that, endlessly, books on LEGO mention the pain of stepping on a brick (and of course *The LEGO Movie 2* includes such a moment). The books celebrate the delight of LEGO creativity but can't help reminding the reader of the obdurate quality of the brick and its noncuddly persistence in hurting humans.

11. For *Happy Feet* (2006), Animal Logic, the digital effects company that later did the animation for *The LEGO Movie*, "solved" the problem of animating people in much the same way that *The LEGO Movie* does—by simply shooting them live.

12. The 1944 Raggedy Ann cartoon short *Suddenly It's Spring* offers a unique variant on the absent human: here, instead of being out of the room, the doll owner is an extremely ill child, close to death it would seem. Bedridden, she has lost consciousness, and this allows the dolls, when they come to life, to converse among themselves and figure out what they need to do to save her (namely, call on nature to help out).

13. Two installments of *The Twilight Zone* offer very wistful representations of the existential crisis of discovering you're just some sort of figurine. The famous "Five Characters in Search of an Exit" presents the dismal tale of a hobo, clown, ballerina, bagpiper, and military officer finding themselves, with no memory of how it happened, in a deep and smooth cylinder of some sort: they eventually manage to climb up, only to fall to the ground (the cylinder was, it turns out, a bin of toys) and freeze into the inanimate children's dolls they in fact have been from the start: here, the move into the presence of humans takes any animation (life, that is) away from toys. Even more poignant is the episode "The After Hours." A young woman has some strange encounters with a few of the personnel of a department store, especially a salesperson on the mysterious

ninth floor. When she's locked by accident in the store over-
night, mannequins come to life (including that salesperson)
and remind her that she's forgotten she is a mannequin herself, let out for an allotted one-month clandestine vacation
amongst humans. Avowing that the human world she's just
visited was wonderful, the young woman begrudgingly accepts
her fate, and she is next seen as a frozen figure back on display
in the store. Rod Serling's voice-over suggests we ask if we
know what it means to be human—both for ourselves and in
regard to the seemingly human figures around us everyday
who might be mannequins.

14. In *The Place of Play: Toys and Digital Culture*, Maaike Lauwaert traces how suburbanization moved a great deal of children's play into the space of the private home (and to special
sites within the home, such as a playroom) and makes the
intriguing suggestion that LEGO in particular were most
appropriately seen as indoor play items, given their small scale
(they risked being lost in the great outdoors), susceptibility to
dirt (which could interfere with the elements locking together
smoothly), and even the cold outdoors of their origin country,
Denmark. See Lauwaert, *The Place of Play: Toys and Digital
Culture* (Amsterdam: Amsterdam University Press, 2009), 54.

15. Sarah Herman, *A Million Little Bricks: The Unofficial History
of the LEGO Phenomenon* (New York: Skyhorse Publishing,
2012), xii; Robertson, *Brick by Brick*, 13–14.

16. Maaike Lauwaert, "Playing Outside the Box: On LEGO Toys
and the Changing World of Construction Play," *History and
Technology* 24, no. 3 (2008): 225.

PRODUCTION HISTORY, PART 1

1. For Wilfert's take on the movie's inception and how The LEGO
Group moved toward involvement in feature film production,
see the 2014 interview with her at MIPCOM, the very big
convention on entertainment marketing held at Cannes each
year, youtube.com/watch?v=IFMR9s0WTb8.

2. Email from Dan Lin via his staff, July 18, 2019.

3. Ibid.

4. A number of websites link to the early script versions: see, for instance, screenplaydb.com/film/scripts/lego.pdf.

5. See Germain Lussier, "Film Interview: Phil Lord and Chris Miller Talk Visuals and Merchandising in 'The LEGO Movie,'" slashfilm.com, February 4, 2014, slashfilm.com/film-interview -phil-lord-and-chris-miller-talk-visuals-and-merchandising -in-the-lego-movie.

6. Phil Lord, email to author, October 27, 2019.

7. A good first place to start constructing the history of LEGO's involvement in moving-image culture is Sara Herman's *Brick Flicks*, a primer on how to make LEGO movies but also a general history of LEGO moviemaking. See Herman, *Brick Flicks: A Comprehensive Guide to Making Your Own Stop-Motion LEGO Movies* (New York: Skyhorse Publishing, 2014).

8. *Star Wars* was one of the many intellectual properties that Warner Bros. licensed for appearance in *The LEGO Movie*. There was some worry that when the very proprietary Disney finalized its acquisition of LucasFilm, it wouldn't agree to the Star Wars licensing, so a deal was rushed through between Warner and LucasFilm. Indeed, Disney refused to allow its own *Prince of Persia* film to be referenced, even though director-writers Phil Lord and Chris Miller wanted to do so in their movie. See Steven Zeitchik, "'LEGO Movie' Directors Really Wanted 'Prince of Persia' in Film," *Los Angeles Times*, February 13, 2014.

9. Herman, *Brick Flicks*, 9.

PRODUCTION HISTORY, PART 2

1. Keith Scott, "Australia," in Jerry Beck, ed., *Animation Art: From Pencil to Pixel, the Illustrated History of Cartoon, Anime and CGI* (London: Flame Tree Publishing, 2004), 262.

2. A sharp overview of Animal Logic's work on the film can be found in Ben Goldsmith's essay "Is Everything Awesome? *The LEGO Movie* and the Australian Film Industry," in *A*

Companion to Australian Cinema, edited by Felicity Collins, Jane Landman, and Susan Bye (Hoboken, NJ: Wiley-Blackwell, 2019), 149–164.

3. For useful background on Hollywood outsourcing of animation work to foreign specialty production houses, see Noon and Malecki, "Cartoon Planet," 239–271. In this essay written just a few years before Animal Logic's work on *The LEGO Movie* but after the success of its first animated feature, *Happy Feet*, the authors chronicle how, from the farming out to low-cost foreign firms of the uncreative handwork of frame-by-frame drawing (especially backgrounds) for films conceived and preproduced in Hollywood, there was a shift to the use of offshore firms for the much more creative labor possibilities (but also risks) of high-level CGI feature animation (the Hollywood production company would still conceive the film and its visual style, but it was now the foreign firm that had to manufacture the look). The result is a situation in which "the local industry achieves critical mass and begins to hold its own as a major player in film production. . . . The key indicator of expertise is the ability to produce a feature film, which requires finance as well as talent" (261–262).

4. Foreign locations can also, of course, be chosen not for their distinctiveness but for their genericness—the possibility that they can be made to look like other places (Toronto as New York, for instance) or like any anonymous place whatsoever.

5. In this case, the attempt failed. See Danks, "South of Ealing: Recasting a British Studio's Antipodean Escapade," *Studies in Australasian Cinema* 10, no. 2 (2016): 1–14.

6. See Danks, "'Something Short of Fascinating': Re-examining Fred Zinnemann's *The Sundowners* (1960)," *Screening the Past* 43 (April 2018), screeningthepast.com/2017/12/something-short-of-fascinating-re-examining-fred-zinnemanns-the-sundowners-1960.

7. Scott, "Australia," 262–265.

8. For background, see Ben Goldsmith, Susan Ward, and Tom O'Regan, *Local Hollywood: Global Film Production and the Gold Coast* (Brisbane: University of Queensland Press, 2010).

9. For some background, see Nick Herd, *Chasing the Runaways: Foreign Film Production and Film Studio Development in Australia, 1988–2002* (Sydney: Currency House, 2004).

10. See Nalbandian's comments in 2017 in Animal Logic's submission to the Australian Parliament's House Standing Committee on Communications and the Arts in its inquiry into "Factors contributing to the growth and sustainability of the Australian film and television industry." Submission 113 at aph.gov.au/Parliamentary_Business/Committees/House/Communications/AustralianfilmandTV/Submissions.

11. A much-noted scholarly essay on the economics of effects companies centers on the paradox of the Los Angeles–based firm Rhythm and Hue winning an effects Oscar for *Life of Pi* at the very moment the company was going bankrupt from a lack of regular assignments. See Michael Curtin and John Vanderhoef, "A Vanishing Piece of the Pi: The Globalization of VFX Labor," *Television and New Media* 16, no. 3 (2015): 219–239.

12. See screenaustralia.gov.au/funding-and-support/producer-offset/location-and-pdv-offsets.

13. And of course digital effects can also refashion real-life locations into fantasy: for instance, mashing live-action and CGI, the 2019 toy-derived *Pokémon Detective Pikachu* presents in realistic imagery a made-up place, Rhyme City, that mixes recognizable elements from many actual world cities (for example, Rhyme City seems somehow to include London's so-called "Gherkin" skyscraper).

14. See "fxguidetv #186: *The LEGO Movie*," February 7, 2014, fxguide.com/fxguidetv/fxguidetv-186-the-lego-movie; and Ian Failes, "Brick-by-Brick: How Animal Logic Crafted *The LEGO Movie*," February 7, 2014, fxguide.com/featured/brick-by-brick-how-animal-logic-crafted-the-lego-movie. The video interview includes tantalizing glimpses of monitors on which we can see scenes from *The LEGO Movie* before all the rendering and effects had been completed.

15. Richard L. Florida, *The Rise of the Creative Class, and How It's Transforming Work, Leisure, Community, and Everyday Life* (New York: Basic Books, 2002).

16. See the comments to Amid Amidi, "Let's Talk About the Animation in 'The LEGO Movie,'" *Cartoonbrew*, February 5, 2014, cartoonbrew.com/cgi/lets-talk-about-the-animation -in-the-lego-movie-95781.html.

17. See the technical paper by Animal Logic staffers Bryan Smith, Daniel Heckenberg, and Jean Pascal le Blanc, "The LEGO Movie: Bricks, Bricks and More Bricks," SIGGRAPH (New York: ACM, August 10–14, 2014).

18. See the paper by Animal Logic staffers Aloys Baillet, Daniel Heckenberg, Eoin Murphy, Aidan Sarsfield, and Bryan Murphy, "The LEGO Movie: Construction, Animation, and Demolition," SIGGRAPH (New York: ACM, August 10–14, 2014).

PRODUCTION HISTORY, PART 3

1. Cara Buckley, "Soaring Past Low Expectations," *New York Times*, June 6, 2014.

2. For background on Lord and Miller, I have found most useful, especially in the amount of detail, the profile by Adam B. Vary, "The Blockbuster Bromance That Is Taking Over Hollywood," *buzzfeed*, June 13, 2014, buzzfeednews.com/article/ adambvary/phil-lord-christopher-miller-blockbuster -hollywood-bromance.

3. For what it's worth, early scripts for *The LEGO Movie* include pointed commentary on the increasing cultural fascination with members of the Creative Class, even as it doesn't directly use Florida's infamous term. Emmet praises the barista at his coffee shop with the assertion, "You creative types! So delightfully sardonic!" only to receive the rejoinder, "I push one of two buttons on a machine. I would hardly call that creative. I would call that following instructions." See screenplaydb.com/film/scripts/lego.pdf, p. 10.

4. Phil Lord in Robert K. Elder, ed., *The Best Film You've Never Seen: 35 Directors Champion the Forgotten or Critically Savaged Movies They Love* (Chicago: Chicago Review Press, 2013), 27.

5. Lord and Miller also show themselves adept at combining slowness and speed in contrastive amalgams. For instance, the

Jump Street films cut back and forth endlessly between the bulky Schmidt painstakingly going about his business in snail-pace fashion while the slim-and-trim Jenko accomplishes his feats in a zippy manner. Most emphatic—and hilarious—is a sequence in *22 Jump Street* where the two need to sneak into a fraternity house: Jenko acrobatically leaps up over balustrades and from rooftop to rooftop, scored to dynamic music, while Schmidt ascends excruciatingly slowly on a winch (during which the music cuts out and we hear nothing but the inexorable sound of the motor lifting him up).

6. There is a history to be written of how *Saturday Night Live* as a *televised* show geared to topicality and immediacy ("Live from New York!") came, in large part through the cross-media efforts of producer Lorne Michaels, to influence *cinema* comedy across the decades, from, among others, *Three Amigos* and *Spies Like Us*, and so on, with Chevy Chase and Dan Ackroyd and Steve Martin, to *Ghostbusters* (Bill Murray, with an SNL women-filled remake), *Dr. Doolittle* and *Nutty Professor* with Eddie Murphy, Adam Sandler in sports comedies like *The Waterboy* and *The Longest Yard*, Kristen Wiig and Maya Rudolph in *Bridesmaids*, and on and on.

7. See thedartmouth.com/article/1997/01/dicks-house-we -deserve-better.

8. The video can be viewed at Lord/Miller's YouTube site, FineMustaches: youtube.com/watch?v=-NKXNThJ6l0.

9. Over time, however, *Clone High* has become the stuff of legend, a cult classic often looked back on fondly for its scabrous eccentricity within the landscape of TV comedy and animation. For some retrospective reflections on the show by Lord and Miller themselves, see Amos Barshad, "Phil Lord and Chris Miller of 'The LEGO Movie' Look Back on 'Clone High,' Their Cult Classic MTV Cartoon," *Grantland*, February 7, 2014, grantland.com/hollywood-pr ospectus/phil-lord-and -chris-miller-of-the-lego-movie-look-back-on-clone-high-their -cult-classic-mtv-cartoon; and Christian Holub, "15 Years Later: *Clone High* Creators Look Back at Their Cult-Classic Cartoon," *Entertainment Weekly.com*, November 2, 2017,

ew.com/tv/2017/11/02/clone-high-phil-lord-chris-miller
-15-year-anniversary.

10. See Amid Amidi, *Cartoon Modern: Style and Design in Fifties
Animation* (San Francisco: Chronicle Books, 2006).

11. For a sumptuous presentation of the visual style of the film, see
the coffee-table tome by Tracey Miller-Zarneke, *The Art and
Making of Sony Pictures Animation's* Cloudy with a Chance
of Meatballs (San Rafael, CA: Insight Editions, 2009).

12. Early on, Lord and Miller served as two of the many screenwriters for the *very* smutty sex comedy *Extreme Movie* (2008)—
too extreme, it would seem, to even be submitted for a rating
in the United States and released instead as a direct-to-video.

13. Kristopher Tapley, "Inside 'Solo': A 'Star Wars' Story's Bumpy
Ride to the Big Screen," *Variety*, May 22, 2018, variety.com/
2018/film/features/solo-a-star-wars-story-directors-reshoots
-ron-howard-1202817841.

RECEPTION AND AFTER-LIFE

1. See theatlantic.com/politics/archive/2014/04/glenn-beck
-wants-to-escape-the-cutthroat-cynicism-of-politics-by
-making-it-in-the-movie-business/360768.

2. See airwaysmag.com/airlines/turkish-airlines-unveils-safety
-video-in-partnership-with-warner-bros-and-the-lego-movie.

3. The videos can be seen at youtube.com/watch?v=C2hCN
6cVuqM; youtube.com/watch?v=MqbFPn_FwaE.

4. Gregory Wakeman, "Will There Be a LEGO Movie 3? Here's
What We Know," *Metro*, February 7, 2019; metro.us/
entertainment/movies/lego-movie-future-will-arnett
-phil-lord-chris-miller.

5. See, for example, Sandy Schaefer, "LEGO Movie Spinoff
Billion Brick Race Inspired by *Cannonball Run*," *Screen Rant*,
July 16, 2018; screenrant.com/lego-movie-billion-brick-race
-cannonball-run.

6. For one analysis of the *LEGO Movie* sequel's underperform-
ance at the box office, see Scott Mendelson, "Why 'The LEGO
Movie 2' Was Such a Huge Box Office Disappointment,"

Forbes, February 11, 2019; forbes.com/sites/scottmendelson/
2019/02/11/why-the-lego-movie-2-was-such-a-huge-box
-office-disappointment/#259276125d69.

7. Brooks Barnes, "Warner Bros. Lands a Big Fish: Hello Kitty
Goes Hollywood," *New York Times*, March 6, 2019, B3. It
is likewise revealing that in the summer of 2019 when the
live-action, effects-driven *Hobbs and Shaw*, a spin-off from
the Fast & Furious franchise, underperformed ever so slightly
in domestic markets in its first week (but still was number one
at the box office), there was automatic reference in the trade
press to the disappointing revenues for *The LEGO Movie*
spin-offs followed by the sequel, as if what happened there established a citation-worthy precedent in which poorly
performing spin-offs and follow-ups risked harming the
series overall. See, for instance, Anthony D'Alessandro,
"'Hobbs and Shaw' Opens to $60M+ with Even More
Muscle Overseas," *Deadline.com*, August 3, 2019, deadline
.com/2019/08/hobbs-shaw-targeting-4-5m-thursday-night
-early-b-o-read-1202659422.

8. Chris Miller offers some tantalizing hints about the very
ambitious scope of the Spider-Man TV project in an interview with Dominic Patten, "'Spider-Man' Universe TV Series
'Really Special,' Chris Miller Says of Sony Pictures TV Project,"
Variety, August 7, 2019, deadline.com/2019/08/spider-man
-universe-tv-series-details-christopher-miller-phil-lord-sony
-pictures-tv-1202663810.

9. See, for instance, Justin Kroll, "Phil Lord and Chris Miller
Sign First-Look Deal with Universal Pictures," *Variety*,
August 2, 2019, variety.com/2019/film/news/phil-lord-chris
-miller-universal-pictures-first-look-deal-1203289760. At the
very end of 2019, the trade press announced a possible first
project for Lord Miller at Universal: a "bear-driven horror
comedy to be produced between Lord Miller and the filmmaking collective Radio Silence who made the hit film
Ready or Not." See, for instance, Mia Galuppo, "Phil Lord,
Chris Miller Team with 'Ready or Not' Directors for Bear

Horror-Comedy (Exclusive)," *Hollywood Reporter*, December 16, 2019, hollywoodreporter.com/heat-vision/phil-lord-chris -miller-team-ready-not-directors-bear-horror-comedy -1247090.

In an interesting twist to the story of the LEGO film franchise, the very end of 2019 also brought reports that TLG and Warner Animation had decided not to continue their joint effort at LEGO feature filmmaking. TLG, it was said, was looking for other studio alliances, *including Universal*. See, for instance, Amid Amidi, "Everything WAS Awesome: Warner Bros. Has Given Up on LEGO Movies," *Cartoon Brew*, December 20, 2109, cartoonbrew.com/business/everything -was-awesome-warner-bros-has-given-up-on-lego-films -184096.html. In fact, in April 2020, it was announced that the LEGO franchise would indeed move to Universal. See, for instance, Mike Fleming, "Universal, Lego Group Construct Five-Year Exclusive Film Partnership To Create New Movie Franchises," Deadline.com, April 23, 2020, deadline.com/2020/04/universal-lego-group-construct -five-year-exclusive-film-partnership-to-create-new-movie -franchises-1202916170.

LEGO Bibliography

Archer, Neil. "Case Study: *The LEGO Movie*, or, Play Well!"
In *Twenty-First Century Hollywood: Rebooting the System*,
96–103. London and New York: Wallflower, 2019.

Baichtal, John, and Joe Meno. *The Cult of LEGO*. San Francisco:
No Starch Press, 2011.

Essex, Andrew. "The Great Danes." In *The End of Advertising:
Why It Had to Die, and the Creative Resurrection to Come*,
168–174. New York: Spiegel and Grau, 2017.

Goldsmith, Ben. "Is Everything Awesome? *The LEGO Movie* and
the Australian Film Industry." In *A Companion to Australian
Cinema*, edited by Felicity Collins, Jane Landman, and Susan
Bye, 149–164. Hoboken, NJ: Wiley-Blackwell, 2019.

Herman, Sarah. *A Million Little Bricks: The Unofficial History of
the LEGO Phenomenon*. New York: Skyhorse Publishing, 2012.

——— . *Brick Flicks: A Comprehensive Guide to Making Your
Own Stop-Motion LEGO Movies*. New York: Skyhorse
Publishing, 2014.

Hjarvard, Sig. "From Bricks to Bytes: The Mediatization of a
Global Toy Industry." In *European Culture and the Media*,
edited by I. Bondebjerg and P. Golding, 43–63. Bristol, UK:
Intellect.

Hunter, Dan, and Julian Thomas. "LEGO and the System of
Intellectual Property, 1955–2015." *Intellectual Property
Quarterly* 1 (2016): 1–18.

Karmark, Esben. "Challenges in the Mediatization of a Corporate
Brand: Identity-Effects as LEGO Establishes a Media Products
Company." In *Media, Organizations, and Identity*, edited by
Lilie Chouliaraki and Mette Morsing, 112–128. Basingstroke,
UK: Palgrave Macmillan.

Lauwaert, Maaike. "Playing Outside the Box—On LEGO Toys and the Changing World of Construction Play." *History and Technology* 24, no. 3 (2008): 221–237.

Pierson, Ryan. "On the Nonessential Beauty of LEGO." *Special Affects*, March 14, 2014. fsgso.pitt.edu/2014/03/on-the -nonessential-beauty-of-legos-2/#more-3528.

Sarto, Dan. "Supervising Animator Chris McKay Talks The LEGO Movie'" (interview). *Animation World Network*, February 10, 2014. awn.com/animationworld/ supervising-animator-chris-mckay-talks-lego-movie.

Robertson, David C. (with Bill Breen). *Brick by Brick: How LEGO Rewrote the Rules of Innovation and Conquered the Global Toy Industry*. New York: Crown Business, 2013.

Schultz, Majken, and Mary Jo Hatch. "The Cycles of Corporate Branding: The Case of the LEGO Company." *California Management Review* 46, no. 1 (Fall 2003): 6–26.

Wolf, Mark J. P., ed. *LEGO Studies: Examining the Building Blocks of a Transmedial Phenomenon*. New York: Routledge, 2014.

Index

Adult Fans of LEGO, 4, 13, 35, 115

Altman, Robert, 136

Amidi, Amid, 148

Animal Logic, 117, 120–129, 131–132, 165–166, 189n11

Annabelle (horror film franchise), 79

Annie Hall (1977 film), 142

Arnett, Will, 168

Avengers: Endgame (2019), 143

Aycı, İlker, 163

Bachelor Mother (1939 film), 80

Baker, Neil, 184n2

Bambi (1942 film), 14

Barney (PBS children's show), 14

Beck, Glenn, 159

Big Hero 6 (2014 film), 125, 132

Bionicle: The Mask of Light (LEGO DVD movie), 83–84, 111

Blackboard Jungle, The (1955 film), 143

Blade Runner (1982 film), 10, 92–93

Bless the Harts (FOX television series), 169

Blumberg, Barry, 144–145

Blur (animation firm), 99

Bowie, David, 1–3

Bratz (2017 film), 82–83

Brick-films, 113

Brony, 13

Cavell, Stanley, 8

Christiansen, Godtfred Kirk, 96, 104–106

Christiansen, Ole Kirk, 104–106

Chucky (horror film franchise), 79

Clone High (MTV television series), 100, 136, 138, 140, 144–148, 158, 182–183n1

Cloudy with a Chance of Meatballs (1978 children's story), 149

Cloudy with a Chance of Meatballs (2009 film), 100, 142, 148–153, 158

Cooper, Tommy (UK comedian), 108

Danks, Adrian, 118

Dark City (1998 film), 120

Deadpool (2016 film), 48

DeFaria, Chris, 124

De Laurentiis, Dino, 119

Dreams of Toyland (1908 film), 188–189n8

Dumbo (1941 film), 9

"Dumpressive," 130

DUPLO, 51, 54, 66, 69, 74, 107, 154, 167

Ealing Studio, 118
Edward and Friends (LEGO
    television series), 109
Ehrlich, David, 140, 141
Eisenstein, Sergei, 177n4
Eisner, Michael, 144
Elsaesser, Thomas, 10–11
Essex, Andrew, 35
Eternal Square, The
    (1947 film), 85
"Everything Is Awesome" (song),
    23–24, 42–43, 51–54, 60, 68

Fahrenheit 451 (1966 film), 50–51
Ferrell, Will, 74–75, 139, 185n5
Fishburne, Laurence, 46, 49
Florida, Richard, 129
Forte, Will, 136
Freckelton, Grant, 130
Freeman, Morgan, 25–26,
    46, 183n1

Galidor (FOX television series
    and LEO tie-in box set), 111
GI Joe (television series, toys,
    films), 81, 83, 92, 186n3
Glen and Randa (1971 film),
    185n4
Godfrey, Chris, 120
Gondry, Michel, 98
Greenpeace, 183–184n5

Hageman, Dan and Kevin, 98
Hanna-Barbera Australia, 119
Happy Feet (2006 film),
    122–124, 189n11
Hatch, Mary Jo, 36–37
Herman, Sara, 96, 115
Hero (2002 film), 120

Hero Factory (2010 television
    series), 187n4
Hobbs and Shaw (2019 film),
    197n7
Hotel Transylvania (2012 film),
    98, 149
Howard, Ron, 154
Hunter, Dan, 25

Idiocracy (2006 film), 183n3
Indian in the Cupboard, The
    (1995 film), 86

Jaws (1975 film), 151
Johnson, Derek, 13
JoLi, 52
Jump Street 21/22 (film fran-
    chise), 137–138, 142–144,
    153–154, 166, 167, 195n5
Jurassic Park/World (film
    franchise), 187n5

Karen Carpenter Story, The
    (1987 film), 187n4
KGOY (Kids Getting Older
    Younger), 15
Kiddicraft, 106
Kidman, Shawna, 12
Kristiansen, Kjeld Kirk, 108
Kubrick, Stanley, 136

Last Man on Earth (FOX
    television series), 136, 138
Latour, Jason, 28
Lauwaert, Maaike, 97, 190n14
Lawrence, Bill, 145
Lee, Spike, 46
Legend of Bagger Vance, The
    (2000 film), 47

Legend of the Guardians
(2010 film), 124
LEGO Batman Movie, The
(2017 film), 84, 92, 138,
160–161, 169
LEGO Digital Designer
(computer program), 131–132
LEGO Group, The (TLG),
19, 36, 98, 102–103, 107–
109, 111–112, 115, 129, 131,
163, 167
LEGO Mindstorms, 103
*LEGO Movie 2: The Second Part,
The*, 11, 15, 20, 29–30, 51–55,
58, 62, 74–75, 94–95, 107,
116, 165–169
LEGO Movie 4D, The (theme
park short film), 161–163
LEGO Ninjago Movie, The
(2017 film), 63, 160, 164, 169
LEGOLAND Movie World
(theme park attraction), 160
LEGOscape, 132
Leone, Sergio, 125
Lin, Dan, 2–3, 98–100
Little Island, The, 52
Lord, Phil, 24, 27–28, 33, 46,
98–103, 117–118, 125, 128,
130, 133–158, 168–170,
178n8, 181n10, 181n1
"Lottery, The" (Shirley
Jackson story), 54
Lucas, George, 112
LucasFilm, 109–110
Luhrmann, Baz, 122

Manovich, Lev, 8
Matrix, The (1999 film), 10, 29,
46, 48–49, 70, 120, 130

McKay, Chris, 117–118
Miller, Chris, 27–28, 33, 46,
98–103, 117–118, 125, 128,
130, 134–158, 168–170
Miller, George, 120, 122
Mitchell, Mike, 163, 188n6
MOC (My Own Creation), 65
Mondrian, Piet, 105
Morricone, Ennio, 125
Mothersbaugh, Mark, 52–53
Moulin Rouge (2001 film), 122
My Little Pony (toy and film fran-
chise), 13, 83

Nalbandian, Zareh, 120–121,
124, 126
Neeson, Liam, 49, 62
Never Let Me Go (Kazuo
Ishiguro novel), 93
Ninjago (LEGO TV series), 63

Ocean's Eleven (1960 and 2001
films), 67, 185n3
On the Beach (1959), 118

Page, Hilary Fisher, 105–106
Patterson, Shawn, 52
PDV Offset, 122
Planet of the Apes (1968 film),
185n4
Playmobil Movie, The
(2019 film), 92
Pokémon Detective Pikach
(2019 film), 186n4, 193n13
Pratt, Chris, 49, 176–177n4
Proyas, Alex, 119–120
"Puff the Magic Dragon"
(folk song), 85

Raggedy Ann and Andy
  (1941 film), 86–87
Raggedy Ann and Andy
  (1977 film), 73, 86
Ramsey, Peter, 156
Robertson, David C., 18–19, 36,
  56, 96
Robot Chicken (Adult Swim
  television series), 118
Roger and Me (1989 film), 151
Rothman, Rodney, 156
Rudolph, Maya, 74–75, 139

Sarsfield, Aidan, 129
Saturday Night Live (NBC
  television series), 74,
  139–140, 195n6
Scott, Keith, 117, 119
Schrab, Rob, 163
Schultz, Majken, 36–37
Scorsese, Martin, 136
Scott, A. O., 179n11
Seagram Building, 105
Simpsons, The (FOX television
  series), 24–25, 30, 41
Small Soldiers (1989 film),
  94, 185–186n1
Snyder, Zack, 124
Solo (2017 film), 154–155
South Park (Comedy Central
  television series), 30, 148
Sony Pictures Imageworks, 166
Spider-Man: Into the Spider-Verse
  (2018 film), 15, 17, 23, 26–27,
  140–41, 144, 146,
  152, 155–158,166
Star Wars (film franchise), 21, 25,
  56, 64–65, 110–111, 154–155
Star Wars: The Padawan Menace
  (LEGO television special),

112, 126–128, 184n1
Stepford Wives, The
  (1975 film), 54
"Steven Spielberg Moviemaker"
  (LEGO box set), 112–114, 116
Stranger than Fiction
  (2006 film), 185n5
Suddenly It's Spring (1944 film),
  189n12
Suddleston, Geoff, 149
Sundowners, The (1960 film),
  118–119
"System of Play" (LEGO
  construction principle),
  4, 96–97, 106, 109

"Teddy" Bears, The (1907 film),
  80–81, 85
Thomas, Julian, 25
Thomas the Tank Engine
  (television series), 81–82, 84
Tiomkin, Dimitri, 119
Toy Story (film franchise),
  86, 88–89, 91, 94
Transformers (film franchise), 81
Traveller's Tales (game
  company), 3
Trolls (2018 film), 187–188n6
Truman Show, The (1998 film),
  10, 54, 93, 177n4
Turkish Airlines LEGO safety
  videos, 163–165
Twilight Zone, The
  (1960s television series),
  79, 189–90n13
2001: A Space Odyssey
  (1968 film), 105

UglyDolls (2019 film), 73, 90,
  178–199n9

Village Roadshow, 32, 119–
    120, 122
Vzpoura hraček
    (1946 Czech film), 79

Warner Animation Group, 3, 32,
    98, 103, 124
Warner Bros., 3, 32, 89, 103,
    118–120, 122, 124, 163, 169
Warren-Crow, Heather, 177n5
Wilfert, Jill, 99
Williams, Mark, 140
Wrinkle in Time, A (Madeleine
    L'Engle novel), 54

Zardoz (1974 film), 185n4
Zhang Yimou, 120–121
Zinnemann, Fred, 119